LIBRARIES & GARDENS

*ALA Editions purchases fund advocacy, awareness, and accreditation programs
for library professionals worldwide.*

LIBRARIES & GARDENS
* GROWING TOGETHER *

CARRIE SCOTT BANKS | CINDY MEDIAVILLA

CHICAGO | 2019

CARRIE BANKS has worked with and on behalf of children with disabilities since high school. Taking over Brooklyn Public Library's Inclusive Services in 1997, she created their gardening program in 1999. Ms. Banks taught inclusion at Pratt Institute from 2013 to 2015 and conducts inclusion trainings across the United States and Canada. She has had many roles in ALA: ASGC-LA (Association of Specialized, Government and Cooperative Library Agencies) board member, committee member and chair, program organizer, and co-drafter of resources and tools for serving people with disabilities. Her substantially revised edition of *Including Families of Children with Special Needs: A How-To-Do-It Manual for Librarians* was published in 2014.

CINDY MEDIAVILLA is a retired public librarian who also worked for the California State Library for ten years. She is currently a library consultant, trainer, and author. Her areas of expertise include after-school homework programs, outcomes measurement, community assessment, and the history of California libraries. In 2007, Cindy and her husband converted their home lawns to drought-tolerant California native plant gardens. Their home has been featured on several garden tours, including Theodore Payne Foundation's prestigious annual tour. Cindy's master's degree and doctorate in library science are both from UCLA.

© 2019 by the American Library Association

Extensive effort has gone into ensuring the reliability of the information in this book; however, the publisher makes no warranty, express or implied, with respect to the material contained herein.

ISBN: 978-0-8389-1855-5 (paper)

Library of Congress Cataloging-in-Publication Data

Names: Banks, Carrie Scott, author. | Mediavilla, Cindy, 1953- author.
Title: Libraries and gardens : growing together / Carrie Scott Banks and Cindy Mediavilla.
Description: Chicago : ALA Editions, 2019. | Includes bibliographical references and index.
Identifiers: LCCN 2018059577 | ISBN 9780838918555 (print : alk. paper)
Subjects: LCSH: Libraries—Environmental aspects. | Libraries and community. | Community gardens. | Library buildings—Environmental aspects.
Classification: LCC Z716.4 .B26 2019 | DDC 025–dc23
LC record available at https://lccn.loc.gov/2018059577

Book design by Alejandra Diaz in the Franklin Gothic and Novecento typefaces.

♾ This paper meets the requirements of ANSI/NISO Z39.48-1992 (Permanence of Paper).

Printed in the United States of America
23 22 21 20 19   5 4 3 2 1

CONTENTS

Acknowledgments vii
Introduction ix

CH 1   **A Brief History of Libraries and Gardens** 1

CH 2   **Demonstration Gardens in Libraries** 7

CH 3   **Learning in Library Gardens** 17

CH 4   **Community Engagement** 31

CH 5   **Library Garden Design** 43

CH 6   **Planning and Managing the Library Garden** 55

CH 7   **Sustaining the Garden through Funding, Partnerships, and Volunteers** 69

CH 8   **Evaluating Garden Programs** 83

APPENDIX A
A Tour of All the Gardens Mentioned in This Book   93

APPENDIX B
Sample Community Garden Rules, Regulations, and Gardener Agreements   105

APPENDIX C
Sample Volunteer Gardener Application   111

APPENDIX D
Sample Evaluation Report   115

Bibliography   119
Index   131

ACKNOWLEDGMENTS

We have many people to thank for helping make this book possible. First, we want to acknowledge Jamie Santoro, acquisitions editor at the American Library Association (ALA), who knew we'd make a good team and so brought us together to write this book. Thanks, Jamie, for your encouragement and ever-patient guidance as we pulled our manuscript together.

It would be difficult to fully appreciate what's accomplished every day in library gardens without talking to staff or seeing their work firsthand. We are grateful to the many library employees and volunteers who graciously answered our questions and, in many cases, gave us tours of their wonderful gardens at Albuquerque Public Library, New Mexico; the Anythink Libraries, Colorado; Arlington Heights Memorial Library, Illinois; Arlington Public Library, Virginia; Armstrong Browning Library and Museum, Baylor University, Texas; Austin Public Library, Texas; Bibliothèque et Archives nationales du Québec; Boonsboro Free Library, Maryland; Boston Public Library, Massachusetts; Brooklyn Public Library, New York; Brown County Library, Wisconsin; Burlington Public Library, Ontario, Canada; Carnegie Library of Pittsburgh, Pennsylvania; Centennial College Library and Academic Facility, Ontario, Canada; Chicago Public Library, Illinois; Cleveland Public Library, Ohio; Daffodil Valley Elementary School Library, Wisconsin; Davis Bilingual Elementary Magnet School Library, Arizona; Dumbarton Oaks Research Library and Collection, Washington, DC; Fanwood Memorial Library, New Jersey; Forsyth County Public Library, Georgia; Glendale Public Library, Arizona; Gwinnett County Public Library, Georgia; Health Sciences Library, University of North Carolina at Chapel Hill; Hall Middle School Library, California; Huntington Beach Public Library, California; J. Willard Marriott Library, University of Utah; John Trigg Ester Library, Alaska; The Library at The Gardens, Alabama; Leslie F. Malpass Library, Western Illinois University; Long Beach Public Library, California; Mānoa Elementary School Library, Hawaii; Marcia R. Garza Elementary School Library, Texas; Metropolitan State University Library and Learning Center, Minnesota; Mid-Columbia Libraries, Washington; Middle Country Public Library, New York; Mill Valley Public Library, California; Mt. Lebanon Public Library, Pennsylvania; Nahman-Watson Library, Greenfield Community College, Massachusetts; Nashville Public Library, Tennessee; National Institutes of Health Library, Washington, DC; National Library of Medicine, Washington, DC; Northern Onondaga Public Library, New York; Ohio Library for the Blind and Physically Disabled, Ohio; Oakland Public Library, California; Omaha Public Library, Nebraska; Pauma AA'Alvikat Library, California; Placitas Community Library, New Mexico; Portland High School Library, Tennessee; Princeton Public Library, Illinois; R. Howard Webster

Library, Concordia University, Montreal, Canada; Rheinland-Pfalz Library, Germany; Richmond Public Library, California; Rockdale Elementary School Library, California; Sacramento Public Library, California; San Mateo County Library, California; Santa Clara County Library District, California; Southfield Public Library, Michigan; St. George's School Library, Rhode Island; St. Helena Public Library, California; St. Louis County Library, Missouri; Staunton Public Library, Virginia; Surrey Public Library, British Columbia, Canada; Sycamore Public Library, Illinois; Upper St. Clair Township Library, Pennsylvania; Vancouver Public Library, British Columbia, Canada; Washoe County Library System, Nevada; Westbank Libraries, Texas; Westmeade Elementary School Library, Tennessee; and William E. Laupus Health Sciences Library, Country Doctor Museum, East Carolina University, North Carolina.

We are also indebted to Wayne Wiegand, Bernadette Lear, Debra Hansen, and other members of the ALA Library History Round Table for their assistance in identifying the many libraries that had gardens in the past. Thanks, too, to Jill Youngs of Northern Onondaga Public Library's LibraryFarm and Alex Meyers of Westbank Libraries for allowing us to include their garden rules as appendixes, even though both gardens are currently undergoing changes. Joanne Toms of the Glendale, Arizona, Xeriscape Botanical Garden and Gwen Blom of Washington State University's Master Gardeners were also extremely helpful in acquiring photos of their gardens.

Carrie, in particular, gives special thanks to Andrew Nowak, of Slow Food USA; Karl Debus-Lopez and Roxanna Benavides, for sharing her e-mail inquiry with their colleagues; Loren Inglarsh for the grand tour of Western Illinois; Paula Holmes, Lilly Garfield, and Marti Goddard, for helping her find libraries; Barbara Klipper, who helped her find libraries and words; the Master Gardeners of Forsyth, Georgia, Allegheny, Pennsylvania, and Sandoval and Montgomery Counties, Maryland; and, of course, to her husband and son, particularly for their patience.

Cindy thanks her landscape architect, Joel Lichtenwalter, who taught her everything she knows about native plant gardens. She can't believe it's already been eleven years since they converted brown lawns into glorious gardens. Cindy is also most grateful for the never-ending support of her husband, Tim, who accompanied her on the "great California library gardens tour of 2017." She's looking forward to joining him again in their own gardens now that the book is done!

CARRIE BANKS
CINDY MEDIAVILLA
October 2018

INTRODUCTION

Libraries and gardens are natural cousins—they both depend on collective effort, they are bedrocks of our communities, they bring people together, and they require a lot of weeding!
—HEATHER McCAMMOND-WATTS (2015)

Both of us have long been fascinated by gardens. Although Carrie is not a gar-dener herself, she learned to love gardens from her grandmothers, one of whom led a peripatetic life as a minister's wife and always grew a garden in each new city; the other lived in her childhood home and grew vegetables in the backyard, which the family ate fresh or preserved all year long. For Carrie, gardening is about creating an inclusive environment where everyone can come together to engage in and enjoy a common goal. With the proper infrastructure, tools, and design, gardens can provide a level playing field for those with and without disabilities as well as for those who may have never gardened before. As director of Brooklyn Public Library's Inclusive Services Department, Carrie oversaw the development of four inclusive library gardens, including one at the central library. She wrote a manual on inclusive gardening, has given workshops with Brooklyn Botanic Garden educators, and has served on the National Gardening Association's advisory board. Inclusion is her passion. Carrie's experiences and observations, while working in Inclusive Services, provide the basis for several of the examples mentioned in this book.

Meanwhile, in Los Angeles, Cindy's front yard and backyard were beginning to feel the full effect of the California drought when the governor announced statewide watering restrictions. So she and her husband immediately converted their grass lawns into drought-tolerant, California native plant gardens. At the same time, the California State Library, for which Cindy then worked, began awarding federal grants supporting native garden demonstration projects at public libraries. Following up on these projects, Cindy discovered that many libraries now had gardens serving many different purposes. Amazed, she wondered if this might be a good topic for a book. She contacted ALA acquisitions editor Jamie Santoro, who put her in touch with Carrie. We then spent the next two years researching and writing this book.

When telling friends and colleagues that we were writing a book on library gardens, inevitably someone would ask, "Do you mean like the gardens at the Huntington Library?" Well, even though we describe how some libraries are partnering with local botanical gardens, the Huntington, in Southern California, is more an art gallery and museum than a library and so is not included here. Nor are other botanical gardens, unless they have a clear connection to a library.

"What about beauty?" another person asked. "Are you only including the most beautiful library gardens in your book?" Our response, of course, was that all gardens are beautiful in their own way. What's most important here is how the garden helps the library meet its service mission.

DEFINING LIBRARY GARDENS

So what exactly is a "library garden"? Rather than being just part of the surrounding landscape, these gardens are purposely created to extend and enhance the library's role as an information center and community space. Whether an outdoor storytime area or an atrium that invites nature inside, the gardens in this book provide a more experiential element to the library. They can bring photos and written descriptions of plants to life and often help preserve history. Many of these gardens also feed communities and teach community members how to feed themselves. In addition, the green spaces described here, such as living walls and rooftop gardens, help the library achieve energy efficiency and may, in turn, serve as demonstration projects for the rest of the campus or the community.

In this book, we offer multiple examples of the many different roles library gardens play, everything from STEM (science, technology, engineering, mathematics) laboratories to providers of medicinal herbs. All of these gardens take their libraries in new and exciting directions. Plus we've included gardens from all types of libraries: public, school, academic, research, historical, special, prison, tribal, military, and subscription. At least one library garden is represented from every continent, except Antarctica, though Carrie did manage to find a library at Scott Base, New Zealand's permanent Antarctic research station, where interior photos reveal at least one short palm tree and a host of potted plants! For those of you hoping to visit the various sites we've written about, we compiled a "garden tour" list of every library garden mentioned in this book (see appendix A). Arranged geographically by region and alphabetically by state, the list includes library addresses as well as websites.

ABOUT THIS BOOK

Despite their natural kinship, very little has been written about libraries and their gardens, even though gardens have been an important part of the library landscape for more than a century. This book not only introduces library gardens into the professional conversation; it also celebrates the role of gardens in today's libraries. Many of these sites have won national as well as local awards, and all accomplish their goals successfully every day. We cite numerous case studies here and also provide advice on what to consider before launching a library garden of your own.

After presenting a brief history of libraries and gardens in chapter 1, we describe a variety of "demonstration gardens" in chapter 2, including medicinal and herbal gardens, native plant gardens, xeriscapes, and gardens as wildlife habitats. We also look at the important role Master Gardeners play in creating and maintaining library gardens. Chapter 3 examines gardens as learning environments, including those created to support library STEM programs. We also introduce the principles of Multiple Intelligences, Universal Design for Learning, and Culturally Relevant Education as viable frameworks on which to design library gardens and educational programming.

In chapter 4, we investigate the many ways library gardens engage the community. Food gardens, seed libraries, sensory gardens, and space for active play are all represented here, as are prison garden programs. We discuss garden design in chapter 5, including green spaces that meet environmental requisites as well as provide attractive architectural features. We also describe outdoor reading areas.

No service should be offered without first considering its impact on the rest of the library, and so chapter 6 is about planning and managing the library garden. We ponder and discuss several questions, including who will maintain the garden, what legal restrictions might exist, how to make the space accessible, which plants to grow, and what challenges lie ahead. And, of course, no library program can flourish without funding, partnerships, and volunteers, which we consider in chapter 7. We end our narrative, in chapter 8, by sharing ideas on how to evaluate the effectiveness of library gardens and the program opportunities they offer.

We hope this book provides readers with a framework that they will then implement in creating their own library gardens. After all, as Cicero once wrote, "If you have a garden and a library, you have everything you need."

CHAPTER ONE

A Brief History of Libraries and Gardens

G ardens have long been associated with knowledge and creativity. In China, early "scholar gardens" offered a carefully curated retreat where intellectuals could escape the hustle of daily life and indulge in more creative pursuits (Morris 1983, 79–81). One such scholar, the eleventh-century Confucian Ssu-ma Kuang, called his outdoor retreat the "Garden of Solitary Pleasure," where he fished, gathered medicinal herbs, tended his flowers, and trimmed bamboo. The garden was also home to his private library, where he collected thousands of manuscripts in order to study and contemplate the origins of the universe. Here is where Ssu-ma Kuang sought inspiration to write his masterwork *Comprehensive Mirror for the Aid of Governance (Tzu-chih t'ung chien)*, an encyclopedic tome spanning thirteen hundred years of history.

Meanwhile, on the other side of the globe, early botanical gardens began taking root in Europe. Although Theophrastus, known as the ancient Greek "father of botany," had classified and organized Aristotle's Lyceum garden into a living library hundreds of years before, more contemporary examples of scientific botanical gardens did not truly emerge until the sixteenth century. Usually attached to universities and medical schools, these types of gardens were used primarily by scholars and teachers. Scientific, as well as economic, interests were further piqued by plants brought back to Europe from other continents during the age of exploration (Spencer and Cross 2017). No surprise, then, that the European colonists who settled in North America were fascinated by the flora of their newly adopted homeland. In 1728, a Quaker botanist, John Bartram, planted what would become the United States' oldest surviving botanical garden. Today, the John Bowman Bartram Special Collections Library, in Philadelphia, houses an extensive collection of documents and materials related to Bartram's Garden and the early development of the field of botany.[1]

TWENTIETH-CENTURY LIBRARIES

As cities grew and industrialization flourished, space for public parks and gardens became more precious. To compensate, librarians in some larger American cities began offering their services outdoors. Garden reading rooms built atop public libraries were especially popular. As New York Public Library (NYPL) director John Shaw Billings explained, rooftop spaces were created "to provide in densely populated neighborhoods adequate places for reading and study in the open air, where such opportunities are otherwise very limited" ("Report of the Director" 1906, 511). One of the first such reading rooms was built as part of NYPL's Rivington Street branch, located in New York City's Lower East Side (Greenberg 2003, 182–183). Opened in 1905, the rooftop garden, which was used from May 1 until mid-October, had a tile floor, iron railings, wooden tables, and an awning. Up to fifty children were allowed to read on the roof during the day, but from 6:00 to 9:00 p.m. the space was reserved for adults only. The roof garden attracted nearly 7,500 readers its first summer. Soon other NYPL branches, including Hamilton Fish Park, William Seward Park, St. Gabriel's Park, and Columbus, boasted of having rooftop gardens. Promotional posters enticed community members by promising, "After the heat and noise of the day's work, why not enjoy the books and magazines on the roof of the library nearest to you." Thousands of people took advantage of this offer until 1920, when the service was discontinued.

Los Angeles Public Library (LAPL) also provided a rooftop garden at its temporary quarters in city hall. But unlike NYPL, which offered the service only during the summer, LAPL's outdoor reading room was open year-round. As naturalist and city librarian Charles Lummis (1907) bragged in his 1905–1906 annual report, "Our roof garden, which has interested librarians throughout the world, would be widely

Rivington Street Library roof garden, New York City, ca. 1919

Photo credit: Library of Congress

copied if our climate could be borrowed with our example" (24). He then went on to describe, in great detail, the various plants occupying the 6,300-square-foot space: a "19-foot Dracena, and a 23-foot Crépe Myrtle," 100 rose bushes, a 55-foot heliotrope hedge, geraniums, grapevines, wisteria, honeysuckle, and 18 trees, including palms, cherimoya, alligator-pear, maple, oleander, and several varieties of fruit (25). A third of the garden space was reserved for women, with the rest open to men, many of whom were smokers. "We cannot help their smoking, but we can help their reading," Lummis reported (25). "[I]t seems to me a sin to discourage from library privileges those who would enjoy them more if the library were a little more homelike" (26). Some 200 users visited LAPL's rooftop reading room every day.

Outdoor reading areas became especially prevalent during the Great Depression when thousands of unemployed people spent their days at local public libraries. LAPL, for instance, provided books, tables, and umbrellas on the east lawn adjacent to its new central library, opened in 1926 in downtown Los Angeles (Keagle 1938, 539–40). In addition, Works Progress Administration (WPA) employees were tasked with taking magazines and books to Pershing Square, a park located two blocks from the main library, as well as to Lafayette Park near the Felipe de Neve branch. Over 56,000 items were circulated from all three outdoor reading rooms during the 1937–1938 fiscal year (Greenberg 2003, 187).

Public libraries in Cleveland, Philadelphia, and Montclair, New Jersey, also offered outdoor reading areas during the 1930s. Perhaps the best-known garden library of this period was the Reading Room, located in Bryant Park just outside NYPL's mid-Manhattan facility at Fifth Avenue and Forty-Second Street. Described by *New Yorker* magazine as "an eccentric little branch," the Reading Room opened in August 1935 when the head of NYPL's extension division, Ruth Wellman, and four WPA workers set up and staffed a white metal table, shaded by a blue and yellow umbrella, and two carts stocked with books and magazines ("Park Sitters Shun Open-Air Library" 1935; Wellman 1936). Slow to catch on, the service, which was offered through mid-October, Monday–Saturday, from 10:00 a.m. until 7:00 p.m., soon became popular with unemployed men and local office workers. Nearly 10,000 items were borrowed in 1935. Circulation increased to 65,000 items the following year, prompting the library to offer the Reading Room every summer until 1944 (Greenberg 2003, 184–186). Although originally discontinued during World War II, the service was rebooted in 2003 in partnership with the Bryant Park Corporation. The current Reading Room offers an eclectic selection of books, periodicals, and newspapers; movable furniture; children's services; and lunchtime programs (Alliance for the Arts 2015).

Gardening assumed an especially patriotic purpose in the 1940s when home front families voluntarily contributed to the war effort by growing their own food. Even libraries cultivated what were known as "victory gardens." "During World War II, the County Library staff had a victory garden in the space under young trees which grew in the dividing strip in the parking lot in back of the Library," San Bernardino County Library children's librarian Dorothy Traver (n.d.) recalled. "We had a large selection of herbs and salad vegetables, although I think zucchini was the most prolific crop" (7). Those who worked in the garden received free produce; everyone else had to pay. "It [was] a fairly common sight after working hours and on Saturday afternoons and Sundays to see librarians in Levi's and other suitable garb at work on their spring garden in the library's back yard," county librarian Carma Leigh related many years later (Mediavilla 2000, 140).

Some libraries even provided garden food to their communities. Dumbarton Oaks, a former Washington, DC, residence that became a research library in the early 1940s, turned the family vegetable patch into a victory garden (Dumbarton Oaks Archives 2017). The surrounding grounds were made available for various relief functions, and the library hosted two buffet suppers for convalescing soldiers in 1944. Head gardener James Bryce conducted on-site demonstrations to teach members of the American Women's Voluntary Services and other local citizens how to plant a victory garden; topics included soil preparation, seed sowing, fertilization, and irrigation (Dumbarton Oaks Archives 2017). Other libraries across the country also provided programs on how to grow and preserve produce during wartime. Library books such as *Food Gardens for Defense*, *Gardens for Victory*, and *Grow Food for Your Family* were in high demand (Becker 2005, 84).

This connection between libraries and gardens continued well after the Second World War. In Fitchburg, Massachusetts, teens erected a memorial in the library's garden to recognize European cities where books had been deliberately destroyed during the war ("Pupils Shun Movies and Gum" 1947). Elsewhere, garden centers began popping up inside public libraries. One such center was staffed and sponsored by the Horticultural Society of Chicago, which displayed gardening books in the central library's lobby and held lectures throughout the spring and summer; center staff also answered gardening questions ("Seventy-Fourth Annual Report" 1946, 25). Meanwhile, in Winfield, Kansas, the local garden club was asked to set up a gardening center in the library's basement after sponsoring a successful flower show there; proceeds from the show were used to buy gardening books that were housed on shelves "painted apple green to form a pleasant harmony" with the basement's pale peach-colored walls ("Of Library Activities in Kansas" 1947).

By the 1950s, most American architects had assumed a more modern approach to building design, eschewing ornamentation in favor of clean lines and an appreciation of nature. New libraries built during this period often embraced an indoor-outdoor midcentury sensibility. Atriums, open spaces, and floor-to-ceiling windows were common features. Two stellar examples of this architectural style are the Washoe County Library in Reno, Nevada, and Huntington Beach's central library in California. Described as "a wonder to behold" (Robison 2014), Reno's Washoe County Library was built over and around an amazing garden that extends from the ground floor up two stories. Rising from the garden are what one writer called "elevated 'mushrooms' . . . ringed with planter boxes spilling greenery over the sides" (Robison 2014). When seated on these circular reading areas, visitors hover two or three stories above the library's foliage. No wonder the Reno branch was recently named one of six libraries with the "coolest internal space" (Robison 2014). The library's garden contains some thirteen hundred items, including standard corn plants, spider plants, philodrendrons, a forty-foot-tall ficus tree, and a four-story avocado tree donated when it was barely more than just a pit (Pierce 2004). As architectural historian George E. K. Smith (1981) once wrote, "it is difficult to know whether to classify this building as a library or as a botanical garden" (vi). The branch received the American Association of Nurserymen's Industrial Landscape Award, shortly after it opened in 1966, and is listed in the National Register of Historic Places. According to former director Arnold Maurins, the building and its garden reinforce the library's "role in the community as a place where creativity is fostered and where people are connected, not only with information and ideas, but also to an authentic sense of place" ("Washoe County Library Listed" 2013).

Equally significant is Huntington Beach's central library, which opened in 1975. Designed by Dion Neutra, son of the renowned midcentury architect Richard Neutra, the library sits on the edge of a park, where it originally appeared to be floating on a reflecting pool that has since been drained. The water theme continues inside as fountains and a large interior pool help to muffle ambient noise. Lush potted plants encircle the five-story bookstack area, while fiddle-leaf fig trees reach up from the ground level. One visitor affectionately described the library as "a greenhouse or botanic garden" (Bradley 2016). "I . . . wanted people to feel like they were inside of a park," Dion Neutra explained during the building's fortieth anniversary. "It's very soothing when you have all of these aspects of nature incorporated in the design. All of the glass and all the greenery really puts you in contact with nature when you're in here" (Epting 2015). Indeed, as one architectural expert noted, "Neutra's modern approach brings the outside in. . . . It is an ideal space to relax with a book or sit down for a focused work/study session" (Le 2018).

LIBRARY GARDENS TODAY

As we describe in the following chapters, today's library gardens serve many functions. Rooftop gardens not only provide space for users to enjoy nature; they also help to cool library facilities and improve air quality. Library-sponsored community gardens allow residents to exercise their green thumbs while growing food to donate to needy neighbors. And demonstration gardens, designed to show adults how to grow native and pollinator plants, also serve as excellent outdoor classrooms where youngsters can learn basic scientific principles. But perhaps even more important, library gardens encourage community members to connect with one another as well as with nature. "There's a social aspect to community gardens," one Tampa Bay resident explained while pulling herbs at the New River Branch Library's garden in Pasco County, Florida. "It's a great opportunity to meet and share ideas with other gardeners" (White 2016).

NOTE
1. Bartram's Garden, "Access Our Library by Appointment," http://bartramsgarden.org/about/research.

CHAPTER TWO

Demonstration Gardens in Libraries

Although some might argue that all successful gardens demonstrate effective horticultural techniques, a true demonstration garden is one that's specifically designed and maintained to teach gardening principles and practices. Demonstration gardens can be as small as a single bed of related plants or appear as "a series of gardens" representing several different ideas and practices (Glen et al. 2013). While some horticulturists posit that a demonstration garden simply "proves that something is possible," others insist that an educational component, such as classes or tours, be included. Demonstration gardens differ from "display gardens" in that the latter are designed to look good all the time (Marin Master Gardeners 2018; Department of Horticulture n.d.). Not so with demonstration gardens: At the Tony Hillerman Library in Albuquerque, for instance, real-life plant mold and other gardening threats are considered "teachable moments" to be used by volunteers in advising visitors how to treat natural dangers. Indeed, a team of horticultural experts in North Carolina found that people often learn something just by strolling through a demonstration garden (Glen et al. 2014).

When designing a demonstration garden, researchers recommend the following approaches:

- Developing gardens around educational themes, such as food production, water conservation, and right-plant–right-place principles
- Facilitating self-directed learning by labeling the plants and making available brochures and subject-relevant webpages that inform visitors about the garden
- Encouraging participants to reflect on their garden experience by offering tours, demonstrations, and hands-on opportunities
- Evaluating the educational outcomes of demonstration gardens, especially as relates to changes in attitude and reinforced learning (Glen et al. 2014)

As we discuss throughout this chapter, several library demonstration gardens meet many of these criteria.

MEDICINAL GARDENS

Predating modern pharmaceutical production, medicinal gardens—also called apothecary or physic gardens—have been a main source of medicine for most of human history. Documents from China and Africa record the use of therapeutic plants as far back as the twenty-eighth century BCE. During the Middle Ages, monasteries served as medical schools where trained herbalists contributed to manuscripts that were copied by monks in the scriptorium, a precursor to libraries. Today, herbs remain a dominant source of medicine worldwide. The United Nations estimates that 80 percent of Africans rely on traditional herbal medicine, and in China, herbs played a significant role in controlling the severe acute respiratory syndrome (SARS) epidemic of 2003 (Tilburt and Kaptchuk 2008). Other nations also use plants as part of traditional or alternative therapies. Ginger for upset stomachs, feverwort for fever, poppies for pain, moss for bleeding, thyme as an antiseptic, dang dui for muscle relaxation, soy for menopause, and tea for energy are just a few examples still commonly used.

Several academic libraries currently maintain medicinal gardens as part of historical collections or as demonstration gardens. The Country Doctor Museum (CDM), part of the history collection of East Carolina University's Laupus Library, has its own medicinal garden modeled on the Botanic Garden of Padua, the oldest university garden in Europe and a UNESCO (United Nations Educational, Scientific and Cultural Organization) World Heritage site. The CDM garden is at the heart of the museum's mission of portraying artifacts relevant to the practice of medicine from the late 1700s through the first half of the 1900s. All of the garden's herbs would have been used during the nineteenth century: ageratum for colds, colic, rheumatism, and burns; pomegranate for cancer, heart disease, diabetes, and contraception; southernwood for "female complaints"; and valerian for insomnia. Labels explain the historic use of each plant.

The Sam W. Hitt Medicinal Plant Gardens, part of the Health Sciences Library at the University of North Carolina at Chapel Hill, demonstrates a more modern physic garden filled with medicinal plants currently used in the United States. The garden also serves as a classroom and hands-on outdoor lab for biology students, many of whom are members of the Gardening and Ethnobotany in Academia club, which maintains the garden and its website. The mission of the club is "to unite students with the rich and dynamic realm of plants through teaching, learning, service, and community building and by actively encouraging creativity, scholarship, fellowship, and leadership" (GAEA Project n.d.). Library staff give the students an overview of the garden and its history and provide access to the collection's rare botanical books. Exhibits in the library's lobby showcase the students' work in the garden, while the special collections room features an exhibit on the history of plants grown in the garden. Photos, a list of plants and their uses, and a brief history are available on the Hitt Gardens' website.[1]

The medicinal herb garden of the U.S. National Library of Medicine (NLM) has an international as well as spiritual scope. Planted at the National Institutes of Health (NIH), in front of the NLM, the garden is owned by the library but managed by the Montgomery County Master Gardeners program at the University of Maryland. The plants, which come from around the world, include lion's mane, for its antioxidant and cardioprotective properties; patchouli (*Pogostemon cablin*), used in Asia for snakebites and gastrointestinal disorders; and African blue basil, for coughs, headaches, warts, and kidney malfunction. Interns from the National Center for Complementary and Integrative Health visit regularly, and programs are occasionally offered to the public. One popular program, held in late October, focuses on the benefits of garlic, which is traditionally known for helping to manage high blood pressure, high cholesterol, and coronary artery disease as well as for its ability to ward off vampires! A totem pole enhances the contemplative mood of the NLM garden, eliciting healing in a whole different and spiritual way (Modin 2017). Staff from various NIH facilities use the garden as a respite. One researcher, in particular, enjoys the garden's green space and seeing plants from her home country. Another visitor, who started watering the garden on her way to and from work at the Clinical Center, became a Master Gardener after retiring and continues to volunteer in the garden.[2]

MASTER GARDENERS

The first Master Gardener program was established through Washington State University's extension services, in 1973, to meet the public's unquenchable demand for urban horticulture and gardening advice. A training curriculum was developed to teach the research-based fundamentals of gardening and the safe control of plant diseases, insects, and weeds. Today, all fifty states offer Master Gardener programs through land-grant universities and their cooperative extension departments.[3] People wanting to become Master Gardeners must undergo a requisite number of training hours, pass an exam, and then serve a required number of volunteer hours, either conducting workshops and tours or tending community gardens, before being certified (Langellotto et al. 2015; Gibby et al. 2008).

Like libraries, the purpose of Master Gardener programs is to educate and impart information. It seems only natural, then, that libraries would partner with local Master Gardeners to create and sustain library gardens. After a Boy Scout gardening project in Arlington, Virginia, fell "into disarray," two Master Gardeners took over and rejuvenated what is now known as the Glencarlyn Library Community Garden (Mills 2018; Master Gardeners of Northern Virginia n.d.). Calling itself a "teaching garden," this lovely green space is home to sun and shade perennials, trees, shrubs, vines, bulbs, herbs and medicinals, and an exotics garden, including huge banana plants. All flora are labeled and in one section, designated as a "literary garden," visitors are encouraged to match literature-based plantings to books in the library.[4] Five Master Gardeners currently maintain the grounds and contribute to a regularly updated blog about the community garden.

Located behind Kennewick branch, in Washington, the Mid-Columbia Libraries' demonstration garden is an amazing two-acre space maintained by the Master Gardeners of Benton and Franklin Counties. The grounds are divided into twenty-six distinct themes, including herbs, vegetables, shade trees, a bird and butterfly garden, native plants, a xeriscape garden, roses, a Japanese garden, ornamental grass, and a children's garden. The garden's overall goals are these:

- Showing various types of locally suitable trees, shrubs, and other plants and their use in home landscapes and gardens
- Raising public awareness of sound gardening principles
- Providing a place of beauty and tranquility for visitors of all ages (Master Gardeners of Benton and Franklin Counties n.d.)

The library's webpage encourages visitors to "take a stroll through the amazing gardens, get married under the gazebo, or dash through whimsical fountains."[5] Plants are labeled and Master Gardeners have created an extensive website describing each of the themed areas (Master Gardeners of Benton and Franklin Counties n.d.). Plus each garden has its own audio tour detailing the plants and why they are part of the demonstration project. Visitors are urged to check with the library staff if they need further information. Kennewick's demonstration garden is barrier-free and fully accessible.

NATIVE PLANTS

Native plants are indigenous species that grow in a given region. These include trees, flowers, grasses, and other plants that have developed, occurred naturally, or existed for many years in a particular area.[6] Although naturalists have long been fascinated by indigenous flora, the native plant movement didn't really start until the latter half of the twentieth century, when groups like Wild Ones, California Native Plant Society, Theodore Payne Foundation, and New England Wildflower Society began expressing concern over the preservation of natural landscapes. More recently, climate change and a dramatic loss of wildlife have prompted gardeners to reconsider the value of beautiful but unsustainable non-native plants. When the Landa Library's medieval-themed garden, in San Antonio, New Mexico, was suddenly faced with locally mandated once-a-week watering restrictions, the garden's managers decided to introduce native plants into the mix (Mills 2012). "If there was a Texas native that could be included in [the] beds, we used them," Joan Miller (2015) blogged; "[a]s a result, most of the Color and Beauty beds are full of Texas native plants."

Native flora provide host and nectar plants for pollinators and, unlike turf lawns, help reduce a garden's footprint. Indigenous plants' deep roots also absorb excess rainfall and prevent water from running directly into rivers and streams, thus helping provide clean water for everyone. Native gardens not only beautify the surrounding landscape; they also improve wildlife habitats, limit the use of pesticides and other chemical applications, create a more diverse landscape, reduce maintenance, and provide experiential gardening information.

Akin to native gardening is "xeriscaping," defined as the "practice of designing landscapes to reduce or eliminate the need for irrigation" (National Geographic Society n.d.). Effective xeriscaping is achieved through water-efficient irrigation, such as drips and soaker hoses, and by planting drought-tolerant natives (National Geographic Society n.d.). Started in 1990, the award-winning Xeriscape Botanical Garden (n.d.) at the main library in Glendale, Arizona, has been called one of the best demonstration gardens in the state. The grounds are home to over 400 species of desert-adapted plants, including 250 cacti and succulents, 150 edible and medicinal Southwest natives, and 2 extremely rare Chinese lantern and neem trees. Both of these beauties were named "Great Trees of Arizona" by the Arizona Department of State Lands in 2003. The garden is maintained by the city's water conservation coordinator and a team of Friends of the Garden volunteers (Xeriscape Botanical Garden n.d.).

At the height of California's drought in the early 2010s, the Mill Valley Public Library was awarded a Library Services and Technology Act (LSTA) grant to create a water-wise SmartGarden to demonstrate best practices during water-starved conditions. The library staff's philosophy: "Build it and they will come (learn and apply in their own homes)" (Brenner 2015, 5). And come they did. Not only did more than 500 community members attend the library's mostly hands-on gardening workshops, but 95 percent of attendees went home and applied what they had learned (Brenner 2015, 3). As for the library, a rainwater creek and gardens were created to help slow, sink, and spread storm water as it makes its way to a rain tank. The collected water is then used to sustain a garden of more than seventy varieties of native plants that serve as a habitat for the surrounding ecosystem. Educational signs identify the garden and its significance. The most important byproduct of the project is showing residents what they can do to their own home landscapes to improve the local environment.

Of course, not all native plant gardens are found in the West and Southwest regions of the country. The Charles E. Miller Branch and Historical Center's Enchanted Garden, in Howard County, Maryland, features sixty-five varieties of primarily native plants, including black-eyed Susan, purple coneflower, aster, chokeberry, iris, St. John's wort, holly, and turtlehead (Page 2014). Named after the beloved, but now defunct, Enchanted Forest amusement park on nearby U.S. highway 40, the quarter-acre demonstration garden offers several themed areas: a rose arbor, a pizza garden, a rain garden and streambed, a conifer garden, a pond, a Peter Rabbit patch, and an interactive garden where youngsters learn about nature (Brewer 2014). Plus the library is an official stop on the county's Monarch Waystation Trail, a network of outdoor educational venues that teach community members about butterflies and the benefits of native plants.[7] The library also accepted the Million Pollinator Garden Challenge to encourage the creation and preservation of gardens and landscapes that help revive the health of bees, butterflies, birds, and other pollinators.[8]

WILDLIFE HABITATS

Gardens inevitably attract critters. In fact, many library gardens are specifically designed to attract and support wildlife, including insects, birds, and mammals. Some even go so far as to certify their space as a "wildlife habitat," especially since natural habitats are becoming more and more threatened throughout the world. Threats to natural habitats include agriculture; the development of housing, retail, and industry; water development, such as dams for irrigation or electricity; pollution; and climate change. Though each of these realities affects habitats in different ways, they all end in the same result. Agriculture replaces existing native plants with alien ones that require pesticides and fertilizers, which further attack native fauna. Likewise, urban development destroys existing plants, forcing animals out, and replaces them with buildings and new landscapes (Lehmkuhl 2005, 8). Tourism, resulting from development, provides its own dangers: For example, the coastal nests of piping plover populations are routinely disturbed by people walking, riding off-road vehicles, playing with dogs, and exploding fireworks (U.S. Fish and Wildlife Service 2017, 3). In addition, diverting water from its original location can make the land hostile to native species. Water development can also block migration paths—a well-known problem for salmon in the Northwest region of the United States (NOAA Fisheries 2018).

A related problem is habitat fragmentation, which happens when isolated islands of habitat are created because of land development. A road may bisect a forest or desert, or a house may be built between two natural territories. When this seemingly benign type of change happens, animal populations can become so small that reproduction is compromised by a decreased gene pool (Lehmkuhl 2005). Moreover, as competition for now scarce resources increases, wildlife is forced to travel from one small area to another, exposing them to dangerous conditions. This is a major problem for mountain lions in Northern and Southern California as well as for New Jersey terrapins, many of which are killed by cars while crossing roads that bisect their habitats (Dybas and Kulikowski 2015; Riley et al. 2014; Lasnier 2013).

Gardens can play an important role in mitigating the effects of habitat loss and fragmentation. As natural habitats shrink, gardens can have a positive impact on the wildlife population, especially where large geographic areas have been disrupted. The National Wildlife Federation (NWF) confirms that gardening with native plants and trees helps supply the food chain for insects and other animals that depend on them. Furthermore, wildlife gardens can connect the habitat corridors necessary for migrant species.[9] To become an NWF-certified Wildlife Habitat, a garden must provide sufficient food and water, adequate cover to hide from predators and inclement weather, and enough shelter for animals to raise their young. Plus the habitat must adhere to sustainable practices that ensure an environment that is free from poisonous pesticides and fertilizers.[10] The Laramie County Library in Wyoming, the Mukilteo Library in Washington State, the Irmo Branch Library in South Carolina, and the West Tisbury Library on Martha's Vineyard have all completed the NWF's certification process and host their own Wildlife Habitats.

Another such library is the Mt. Lebanon Public Library in Pittsburgh, Pennsylvania. Designated as a Wildlife Habitat in 2009, its garden is managed in partnership with the Friends of the Library and the local Master Gardeners program, sponsored by the Pittsburgh Botanic Garden. Originally established as a rainwater garden in 2000, the grounds currently embrace three sides of the library. Native plants, which make up about 50 percent of the garden, attract wildlife, such as hummingbirds, rabbits, and the occasional deer. Not only does the garden provide the requisite food; it also offers shelter. Water is available via a pond in the library's courtyard, and the surrounding landscape is free of chemicals. No wonder, then, that this garden at the Mt. Lebanon Public Library was named the "best medium-sized garden" in 2012 by the *Pittsburgh Post-Gazette* (Mt. Lebanon Public Library 2012).

Initially started by the school library media specialist and the physical education teacher, the Westmeade Elementary School garden, in Tennessee, has become the impetus for a school-wide sustainability initiative. In 2013, a group of third-graders spearheaded a campaign to get the garden certified as a Schoolyard Habitat. The process helped the children learn why animals are important and how humans can sustain wildlife.[11] The school's garden is now part of an outdoor classroom where students are encouraged to explore and observe living things.[12] Among the many animals supported by the garden are fledgling bluebirds, a local native species that is endangered.

POLLINATOR AND BUTTERFLY GARDENS

Another equally important natural habitat is pollinator gardens, designed to attract butterflies, bees, hummingbirds, bats, and other creatures whose populations are on a serious decline. As the National Pollinator Garden Network asserts, an increased "number of pollinator-friendly gardens will help revive the health of pollinators across the country."[13] An extensive list of links that help identify appropriate plants to attract pollinators by North American regions is available on the network's website.[14] The U.S. Forest Service (n.d.) also provides valuable advice on how to attract pollinators: gardens should include a damp salt lick (preferably sea salt) for bees and butterflies; nesting places for bees, like a dead tree limb; larval host plants, such as milkweed and butterfly bush; and a hummingbird feeder. But be forewarned: you may have to regularly replace larval host plants since caterpillars eat the leaves on which they hatch, as in Eric Carle's (1994) *The Very Hungry Caterpillar*!

The Princeton Public Library, in Illinois, perfectly illustrates the strategies recommended by both the National Pollinator Garden Network and the U.S. Forest Service. Created in 2014 as part of the U.S. Department of Agriculture's "The People's Garden Initiative" (Starr 2015), Princeton's 2,400-square-foot garden features native nectar and pollen plants, such as milkweed, wild bergamot, pale purple cornflower, rough blazing star, and meadow blazing star, to attract butterflies and Illinois' 450 species of bees. "The main thing was to have a buffet of native flowering plants that native pollinators recognize as food," Ellen Starr, biologist with the Illinois Natural Resources Conservation Service, says.[15] The Princeton garden draws much attention and has been used by the library as an outdoor classroom. "Monarch populations have decreased significantly over the past two decades in part because of the decrease in their habitat," Starr laments. "Our pollinator garden here in Princeton helps us do our part for the monarchs" (Starr 2015).

Butterflies are just one of many pollinators the Princeton library hopes to attract; but not so at St. Louis County Library (SLCL), where butterflies are the main event. In 2012, the library partnered with a community network, called Gateway Greening, to create a butterfly garden adjacent to a twenty-bed community garden at the Prairie Commons branch. The St. Louis Audubon Society helped by selecting the native plants to be included. Further partnerships were forged when the library joined the Missouri Botanical Society's Project Pollinator Initiative to promote an appreciation of all pollinators through education and the creation of gardens. The goal of the initiative is "to educate the public about the importance of pollinators, beyond the familiar bees and butterflies, and to provide demonstration gardens at county parks, libraries and other public venues" (Grant 2017).

In some cases, pollinator habitats can be as small as a single plant. In Brooklyn, for instance, a retiring staff member donated a butterfly bush to the library's Inclusive Services garden. It lived up to its name, the following year, by attracting many different types of butterflies. In such a dense urban environment, butterflies can be a precious gift. As Eve Bunting (1994) captures in her lovely picture book *Flower Garden*,

> Garden in a window box
> High about the street
> Where butterflies

Can stop and rest
And ladybugs can meet (20-21)

Six months after the devastating events of September 11, 2001, people visited the Brooklyn library's garden just to see the butterflies. One woman commented that they reminded her of her recently deceased mother, who believed souls turn into butterflies when people die.

OTHER DEMONSTRATION GARDEN EXAMPLES

One of the most beloved library gardens was started in 1962 when the Albuquerque Rose Society (2017) gained permission to plant a public garden on the property west of what was then the Wyoming branch library (now the Tony Hillerman Library). Within four years, the garden was home to some 680 plants, representing 180 varieties and 23 classes of roses. Renovations in 1995 and 2010 expanded the garden, so that it now surrounds the library, boasting some 1,200 roses, including 400 varieties and 30 different classes. The library owns the property, but society members are responsible for taking care of the plants. The roses are labeled, and people come from near and far to visit the garden. Free pruning demonstrations are held every March and the society distributes a list of roses that grow well in Albuquerque. The society also contributes funds to boost the library's gardening book collection.

An equally special demonstration garden, found in Northern California at the St. Helena Public Library, is home to its own vineyard and the Napa Valley Wine Library Association. Called Barney's Backyard in honor of the association's first president, Bernard I. Rhodes, the vineyard produces eighteen magnums, or about twenty-seven liters, of wine a year from ninety-one vines (Banks 2017). The wine is donated to fund-raisers supporting educational causes in Napa County. Open to the public,

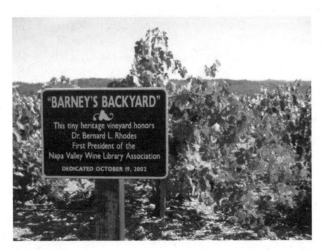

Barney's Backyard vineyard, St. Helena Public Library, California

Photo credit: Napa Valley Wine Library Association

Barney's Backyard was planted in 2002 as a small heritage vineyard, in recognition of local generations of anonymous Mexican and Italian gardeners who cultivated vines and vegetables to feed their families (Allegra n.d.). Because the plants are pruned in a more historically traditional manner, they provide a valuable reference on how to maintain a certain shape and style of vine.[16] A retired vineyardist uses Barney's Backyard to teach hands-on classes on pruning, thinning, veraison, and picking.[17]

NOTES

1. University Libraries, Health Sciences Library, "Sam W. Hitt Medicinal Plant Gardens," University of North Carolina at Chapel Hill, https://hsl.lib.unc.edu/medicinalgarden; Sam W. Hitt Medicinal Plant Gardens, "Plants A–Z," University of North Carolina at Chapel Hill, http://medicinal gardens.web.unc.edu/plants-a-z.
2. M. Musselman, S. Occhipinti, J. Weiss, and P. Kenney, personal communication, February 23, 2018.
3. For a list of Master Gardener programs in North America, see eXtension, "State and Provincial Master Gardener Programs: Extension and Affiliated Program Listings," http://articles.extension.org/pages/9925/state-and-provisncial-master-gardener-programs-extensiuon-and-affiliated-program-listings.
4. Arlington Public Library, "Glencarlyn Branch Library Community Garden: A Teaching Garden," https://library.arlingtonva.us/explore/gardening-and-urban-farming/glencarlyn-garden.
5. Mid-Columbia Libraries, "Kennewick," www.midcolumbialibraries.org/branch/kennewick.
6. Adapted from *Wikipedia*, "Native Plant," https://en.wikipedia.org/wiki/Native_plant.
7. Howard County Library System, "Saving the Magnificent Monarch," http://d3lf1kenz29v4j.cloudfront.net/wp-content/uploads/2015/09/17093653/Monarch-brochure-Sept1.pdf.
8. Howard County Library System, "1M Pollinator Gardens," https://hclibrary.org/locations/miller-branch/enchanted-garden/1m-pollinators-gardens.
9. National Wildlife Federation, "Impact of Wildlife Gardens," www.nwf.org/en/Garden-for-Wildlife/About/Impact.
10. National Wildlife Federation, "Certify," www.nwf.org/Home/Garden-for-Wildlife/Certify.
11. Young Naturalists @ Westmeade, "Help Make Westmeade Tennessee's 1st Sustainability Magnet," www.westmeade.net/our-natural-history-museum.html.
12. Metro Nashville Public Schools, "Westmeade Elementary School," https://schools.mnps.org/westmeade-elementary-school.
13. National Pollinator Garden Network, "Million Pollinator Garden Challenge," http://million pollinatorgardens.org.
14. National Pollinator Garden Network, "Pollinator Resources," http://millionpollinatorgardens.org/resources.
15. E. Starr, personal communication, June 13, 2018.
16. D. Stockton, personal communication, July 4, 2018.
17. C. Martini, personal communication, July 4, 2018.

CHAPTER THREE

Learning in Library Gardens

"When children have regular contact with nature, they learn and grow better," the Middle Country Public Library in Centereach, New York, proclaims. The library goes on to promise that by visiting its outdoor learning space, called the Nature Explorium, youngsters will develop observation and visual-spatial skills, as well as social skills. The experience, they insist, "offers a unique way to connect literacy, learning and an appreciation for nature as a regular part of the library visit."[1] Programs and activities conducted in the Nature Explorium include "Geology Rocks!," "Sunflower Fun," "Let's Salsa" (how to make salsa), "Don't Bug Me" (insects), how to make a "nature book" using found objects, and "Spring Planting."[2]

Gardens are a wonderful incubator of literacy and learning at all ages. For young children, gardens can facilitate vocabulary building, the development of sequencing skills, and conversation. Older children are eager to read seed packets, research needed information, and describe to others what is happening in the garden. English language learners may find common ground and a basis for talking with others as they share their words for produce (e.g., tomatoes, tomates, 番茄, nā'ōmato, and nyanya) and how these items are used in their home countries. Because gardens provide such a broad array of educational opportunities, librarians nationwide are introducing literacy skill building and other types of learning into outdoor settings.

HOW PEOPLE LEARN IN GARDENS

To make learning accessible to as many people as possible, three overarching teaching concepts should guide all library program planning: Multiple Intelligences, Universal Design for Learning, and Culturally Relevant Education. When brought together, these three paradigms create an environment where all learners are welcome.

Howard Gardner (2011), professor of cognition and education at the Harvard Graduate School of Education, postulates that no two people learn in the same way, even though everyone experiences the world using the eight different intelligences outlined in figure 3.1. Though we all have the potential for and indeed use all eight of these intelligences, some are stronger than others in any given individual. Verbal learners, for instance, are most comfortable with words, while logical/mathematical learners see the world through patterns, numbers, logic, and scientific inquiry. Spatial learning covers traditional visual arts and also the relationship between objects and space. Kinesthetic learners, such as dancers, ironworkers, choreographers, yoga instructors, and athletes, process information through movement. Likewise, musical learners acquire knowledge through song (e.g., singing the alphabet). Those who understand things best through discussion and interaction with other people have a strong interpersonal intelligence, but intrapersonal learners are more comfortable with introspection, feelings, and thoughts. Natural learners focus on the natural world to understand things (Gardner 2011). Communicating with learners in the ways in which they feel most comfortable improves the flow of information for everyone. Therefore, though garden programs might appeal most directly to natural learners, adding plant labels, encouraging reflection through garden diaries, and asking visitors to measure the length of leaves will engage more than one type of intelligence.

FIGURE 3.1
The eight Multiple Intelligences

INTELLIGENCE	MODALITY
Verbal	Words
Logical/mathematical	Numbers, patterns, logic, scientific inquiry
Spatial	Art and spatial relationships
Kinesthetic	Movement
Musical	Music and rhythm
Interpersonal	Relationships
Intrapersonal	Self-examination
Natural	Natural world

Source: Adapted from Gardner 2011

Universal Design for Learning (UDL) organizes the eight intelligences so all learners can succeed. These are the four components of the UDL framework:

- Multiple means of representation
- Multiple means of engagement
- Multiple means of expression
- Multiple means of assessment (CAST 2018)

Let's look at how UDL might be applied to learning in a library garden.

Multiple means of representation requires that content be presented in a variety of ways. A garden-based program on pollination, for instance, could start with a handout and lecture (verbal and spatial), followed by small-group discussions in which participants express their feelings about pollinators, like bees and butterflies (interpersonal and intrapersonal). The group would then visit the library garden to observe pollinating insects (natural, kinesthetic, and logical/mathematical). At the end, participants might celebrate pollination by dancing to Nikolai Rimsky-Korsakov's "Flight of the Bumblebee" (musical and kinesthetic).

Having accounted for diverse learners in presenting the material, the next thing to consider is how to engage everyone by connecting the program information to the participants' interests. As engineer, mathematician, and Caldecott Medal–winning illustrator David Macaulay (2009) once said:

> To make sure that no one, child or adult, is truly left behind, all avenues to learning need to be open and available. Whether through drawing, writing, or performance, a person can eventually be led by his own growing enthusiasm to science, mathematics, history, or whatever it is he might need to know. My career is the proof. (10)

The fact that plants lead to the production of food, wood, cloth, paper, rubber, and petroleum should tie the topic of horticulture to almost any interest.

The next step is to allow program participants to express their new knowledge in the ways that are most comfortable for them. A linguistic learner might write a poem, a visual learner might make a video about hand pollination, while a musical learner composes a rap. Assessment of a participant's learning may also be approached in multiple ways, as long as the evaluation examines what is actually known rather than how well the participant takes a test.

If the theories that inform learning are a three-legged stool, then Culturally Relevant Education (CRE) is the third and final leg. CRE is similar to the UDL's multiple means of engagement in that both concepts start with the learner's own experience and interests. As Geneva Gay, professor of education at the University of Washington, says, CRE uses "cultural knowledge, prior experiences, frames of reference and performance styles of ethnically diverse students to make learning encounters more relevant and effective" (cited in Aronson and Laughter 2016, 165). When combined with Gardner's Multiple Intelligences and the UDL, all three educational tools lead to garden environments where everyone can learn. The Brooklyn Public Library's Inclusive Services uses this framework to design programs that are fully inclusive, allowing for a wide variety of skills, abilities, ages, and background knowledge. See, for example, Brooklyn Public Library's lesson plan for a typical program on bean propagation, outlined in figure 3.2.

FIGURE 3.2
Bean Propagation Lesson Plan

ACTIVITY	LEARNING COMPONENT
Read excerpts from *So You Want to Grow a Taco* (Heos 2016).	Verbal, logical/mathematical, spatial
Sing "Everyone Grows" with rhythm instruments and prerecorded chorus.	Musical, interpersonal
Discuss beans and their uses in cuisines around the world.	Interpersonal, verbal
Ask participants to reflect on experiences with beans.	Intrapersonal
Read *The Tiny Seed* (Carle 2009).	Verbal, logical/mathematical, spatial
Pass around fresh and dried beans from different parts of the world.	Kinesthetic, natural
Read *Jack and the Beanstalk* (Kellogg 1991).	Verbal, logical/mathematical, spatial
Sing "Beans in My Ears" with rhythm instruments and prerecorded chorus.	Musical, nonverbal communications, interpersonal (humor)
Show stages of bean growth with 3-D foam puzzle.	Kinesthetic, spatial
Plant beans in cups to take home.	Logical/mathematical, kinesthetic, intrapersonal
Clean up.	Kinesthetic, interpersonal
Write group garden diary.	Verbal, interpersonal, intrapersonal

Source: Brooklyn Public Library

The topic of bean propagation is presented through reading, music, manipulation, and demonstration, tying beans to literature, food, art, and science. In addition, the learners are offered several ways to express themselves through music, discussion, planting, and contributing to a group garden diary. The books read represent different cultures, and in one Mexican-American neighborhood, the program is offered in both Spanish and English.

LITERACY PROGRAMS FOR YOUTH

As librarians increasingly see themselves as educators, they tend to include messages about early literacy in their programs for young children and their caregivers. In 2004, the Association for Library Service to Children (ALSC) and the Public Library Association (PLA) jointly developed a research-based early literacy initiative, called Every Child Ready to Read (ECRR), as a new framework for entertaining little ones while teaching their parents how to support literacy learning at home. Originally, ECRR was organized around six early literacy skills:

1. **Print motivation**—modeling the act of reading, whether it involves street signs, grocery lists, books, and so on
2. **Narrative skills**—the sequencing of stories (e.g., beginning, middle, and end)
3. **Vocabulary learning**—acquiring words through interaction with the environment, playing, conversation, reading, and singing
4. **Phonological awareness**—ability to hear the smaller sounds that distinguish words

ABC Trail at the Nature Explorium, Middle Country Public Library, New York
Photo credit: Middle Country Public Library

5. **Print awareness**—being aware of printed words
6. **Letter knowledge**—recognizing the alphabet (Ghoting n.d.)

As important as these concepts are, it later became apparent that a more practical early literacy approach was more effective, and so the emphasis eventually shifted from the skills themselves to how children acquire them. Thus, the following "five early literacy practices" were adopted in 2010 as ECRR2:

1. **Talking**—encouraging descriptive talking, naming, and conversation around everyday activities
2. **Singing**—learning words through song
3. **Playing**—engaging children in learning through play
4. **Reading**—encouraging literacy by modeling reading habits
5. **Writing**—encouraging literacy through writing (Neary 2014)

A recent three-year evaluation of the program reveals that as a result of ECRR2, many librarians now see themselves as educators. Children, too, see librarians in that role. Moreover, library programming has moved beyond just storytime to include play and fun, an emphasis on STEM topics, and bilingual storytelling. In addition, library staff are focusing more on parents and caregivers and how to model the early literacy practices they hope parents will emulate back home (Neuman, Moland, and Celano 2017).

Although the purpose of the program is to encourage literacy at home, ECRR2 practices have also made their way into library gardens. The Nature Explorium has an alphabet walk with letters posted along a pathway, reinforcing ECRR's letter knowledge skill (Delgado-LaStella and Feinberg 2010). In Forsyth County, Virginia, a StoryWalk based on Eve Bunting's *Sunflower House* was an integral part of the Cumming Library's garden one summer.[3] Children and caregivers follow the laminated book pages that are mounted on posts in the garden until they turn the final corner to find a real sunflower house. Kids and adults alike are delighted to see the book come literally to life, all while learning narrative skills, vocabulary, print motivation, and print awareness.

A growing body of research supports literacy development in gardens. One literature review found that garden-based learning has a positive impact on students' grades, knowledge, attitudes, and behaviors (Williams and Dixon 2013). Another study posited that school gardens "may improve students' attitudes toward school itself—a byproduct of experiential education because school engagement leads to improved academic outcomes" (Berezowitz, Yoder, and Schoeller 2015, 515). Gardens, in fact, may engage young people in ways traditional classroom learning does not. Research shows that students who are disengaged from mainstream teaching benefit most from literacy lessons taught in real-life settings, such as school gardens. As one teacher reported, having students visit the garden "stimulated their brains and the thinking around it and the conversations between each other, so I gave them quiet time at the end of the day . . . to reflect about it . . . and I think that was some of the best writing pieces I had from them all year" (Pascoe and Wyatt-Smith 2013, 38).

At the Apopka Elementary School in Florida, a first-grade teacher and the school librarian developed a six-week garden-based curriculum on plant and insect interactions. Groups of students used books, websites, and the school garden to research a particular bug. A series of increasingly sophisticated writing assignments followed, culminating with three full sentences based on maps the children created. The students also wrote in garden journals. As the unit progressed, the youngsters' writing became more descriptive and specific. "Kids who in September may have written 'The flower is big and pretty' now might write, 'The Dahlberg daisy is 26 inches tall and has leaves with yellow edges,'" the teacher said (Pranis n.d.).

Gardens, whether in schools or public libraries, can also provide increased support for youth with disabilities. For students with learning, developmental, and emotional disabilities, gardens may be that rare place where they can experience success. Educators Joanne Pascoe and Claire Wyatt-Smith (2013) found that students with behavioral problems benefited greatly by spending time in a garden. At one school, kids who exhibited behavioral problems in the classroom suddenly focused when they went outside to the garden. Carrie has witnessed this phenomenon firsthand as well. Ronald, a seven-year-old child with autism, regularly attended the library's gardening program. One day, after listening to a librarian read Lois Ehlert's book *Planting a Rainbow*, he pointed at purple pansies, repeating the librarian's prompt to "point to purple, Ronald." His mother was astonished, saying she had never seen him identify colors before. In the twelve years he attended the library's garden club, Ronald never had a meltdown.

STEM AND LIBRARIES

Other types of learning also occur in gardens. As staff of the Nature Explorium (n.d.) argue, children need outdoor learning opportunities that provide a variety of formal and informal play activities. "Exposure to nature through play leads to exploration and discovery," they contend, "engaging both the physical and mental abilities of the child and providing a holistic approach to learning and [nature] literacy." Furthermore, the need for better science comprehension has become pervasive. As P. B. Dusenbery (2013), executive director of the Space Science Institute in Boulder, Colorado, asserts, "From climate change to threats to human health and access to clean water, the majority of challenges facing society today—and their solutions—are rooted in STEM." Students, he says, must be engaged with and proficient in STEM content and process. "In the 21st Century, a basic understanding of STEM is part of being an informed citizen," he concludes. Library gardens can help provide some of that knowledge.

Concerned that U.S. students were not keeping up with the rest of the world in science, technology, engineering, and math, Congress passed the America Competes Act in 2007, targeting funds for STEM resources and academic programs (Hopwood 2012). Reauthorized in 2011, the White House touted the act as an initiative to enhance STEM education and "raise American students from the middle to the top of the pack and to make sure we are training the next generation of innovative thinkers and doers" (Braun 2011). The importance of STEM learning was further reinforced in 2013 with the adoption of the Next Generation Science Standards (NGSS), a multistate effort to promote science education. The standards encourage students to explore the connections across all four science domains—physical, life, earth and space, and engineering—through inquiry and cognitive, social, and hands-on practice. The purpose is to shift science education from rote memorization of facts to student-driven projects that lead to critical thinking. In New Milford, New Jersey, for instance, the NGSS inspired the high school library to create a garden where students can grow plants and apply agricultural skills. "We have a couple of farms in our community," the library media specialist explains. "We invited in some of the workers from those farms to share their stories and to help ignite that entrepreneurial spirit in our students, along with learning some real-world skills" (Meyer 2018, 35–36).

Although libraries may seem an obvious choice to promote STEM learning, not all librarians are enthused about assuming this new role. One recent study found that "STEM anxiety" occurs when library staff feel unprepared to handle community members' queries about math and science. "How can one engage others in loving science if they themselves don't know or love science, even fear science themselves?" one researcher posited (Baek 2013, 7). Urging that librarians "should not become STEM educators," renowned library proponent R. David Lankes argues that the "key to increasing STEM literacy across all public libraries . . . is to change the perception that librarians have to know everything, or master a topic before they can promote it" (Lankes 2015). Children's librarian Jennifer Hopwood (2012) concurs, encouraging colleagues to include STEM concepts in library programs even if they themselves don't have a science background. In fact, as she insists, "without the formal jargon and training, an informal library program conducted by a nonexpert might relate the information more clearly to students" (56).

In an ALSC webinar, school librarians Alicia Montgomery and Emily Bredberg (2015) remind viewers that libraries foster exploration and, therefore, are the perfect place for STEM learning. Moreover, when kids explore on their own—that is, outside the classroom—they are free to draw their own conclusions. Indeed, as researchers John H. Falk and Lynn D. Dierking (2010) found, the classroom is not where most Americans acquire science knowledge. Instead, science learning more typically happens through informal or "free-choice" experiences in parks, museums, and libraries. "It is exactly because free-choice learning is *not* like school that it has such value," the researchers say (492). For example, when people visit a botanical garden, they not only relax and enjoy their surroundings but also satisfy their intellectual curiosity and gain a better understanding of the natural world. Hobbyists, such as home gardeners, might also acquire a deep, specialized knowledge of science just by honing their craft.

STEM GARDENS

According to Richard Louv (2011a), cofounder of the Children & Nature Network (C&NN), libraries— or "naturebraries," as Louv calls them—are "a perfect place to gently and safely help families connect to nature." Libraries

- can be found in every kind of neighborhood;
- are already community hubs;
- are supported by Friends of the Library groups;
- have existing resources, such as nature books;
- are often more flexible than schools; and
- are known for being safe.

Still, there is always room for improvement, and so Louv suggests that libraries embrace outdoor learning in these ways:

- Promoting family nature clubs (Thielbahr 2011) and providing free toolkits and information, such as C&NN's "Where Nature Meets Story"[4]
- Circulating gardening and other outdoor tools, including fishing poles
- Becoming an information hub of outdoor activities, offering local area maps and brochures
- Developing partnerships with parks departments and garden clubs
- Helping build bioregional identity through collections and programming, including lectures by local nature experts
- Encouraging backyard biodiversity and the "re-naturing" of the community through seed distribution
- Creating outdoor reading and learning centers (Louv 2011b)

Children's librarians, in particular, have long understood the value of outdoor learning. In her early textbook on public library services to children, Effie L. Power (1943) suggests that librarians help youngsters plan "a library (or home) garden" as a noncompetitive, yet fun, summer activity. She also recommends "out-of-door storytelling" (113–14). Today's emphasis on science and learning only strengthens the connection between libraries and nature.

While some libraries support STEM learning through astrology exhibits, 3-D printing demonstrations, architectural design projects, and robotics camps, others look to nature to help community members understand everyday science. Gardens are, after all, "just an older version of Maker spaces," says Adrienne Canino, manager of the LibraryFarm at New York's Cicero Library (Hazlett 2013, 28). Though some programs are more ambitious than others, libraries often offer outdoor STEM learning opportunities as either workshops or hands-on garden experiences. A team of twenty-five teenagers attended library workshops on garden bed construction, soil composition, crop rotations, composting, irrigation installation, and square-foot gardening strategies before designing and building a vegetable garden at the El Dorado County Library in Placerville, California (Amos 2015). Crops included broccoli, onions, radishes, tomatoes, beans, cucumbers, pumpkins, sunflowers, basil, cilantro, and chives, which the teens planted, harvested, and ate. Other library workshops taught them solar cooking, food dehydration, and how to cook with organic food. As a result, they not only learned how to cultivate produce but also how to cook fresh foods and incorporate healthy eating into their daily routines. The project was funded through an LSTA grant.

Two similar grant projects were undertaken in Illinois. In the first, young adult librarian Catherine Barnett started a vegetable garden at the Chillicothe Public Library to spark the community's "sense of observation and wonder" about the environment, sustainable living, and nutrition. Calling themselves the Green Chillis, a group of four teenaged volunteers helped plant and maintain the garden, while the library offered workshops on "herbs for fun and fragrance," edible patio gardens, organic gardening, and other related topics (Green Chillis Garden Club 2011). As Barnett later said, "It certainly has been a learning experience" (Gillespie 2011). The second project, called the STEM Garden, was offered by the Stickney Forest View Public Library District in hopes of encouraging better eating habits (Austen 2016). Local youngsters and their families were invited to help plant a "pizza garden," filled with tomatoes, bell peppers, jalapeños, arugula, basil, parsley, cilantro, and chives. At the end of the grant year, a chef introduced the children to healthy after-school snacks that require little or no adult supervision. Kids learned about gardening and tried foods they had never eaten before.

The Cupertino Library in Santa Clara County, California, features two gardens: one created by and for teens and the other designed specifically for younger children. Initiated by the library's teen advisory board, the Green Teen Garden enlivens a previously barren inner courtyard that has since been converted into an informal reading area. With the help of Master Gardeners and library staff, the teens volunteer for four months, taking turns working in the garden, Thursday through Saturday. Along the way, they learn how to successfully check pH soil levels, turn waste into compost, recycle plastic bottles and newspapers into seedling sprouters, fend off insects, and plant and harvest organic vegetables and herbs. "It feels great to see something as tiny as a seed turn into a big lettuce," teen volunteer Cindy Deng observed (Wilson 2014). Everything grown in the garden is donated to the West Valley Community Services food pantry, so the high-schoolers also learn about service and the importance of meeting the nutritional needs of the community. "It's kind of metaphorical," Deng said, noting how the project's goals quickly expanded. "[The garden] is blossoming and becoming a much bigger project" (Wilson 2014). The Green Teen Garden was recognized as an "innovative project" by the Urban Libraries Council in 2015 (Urban Libraries Council 2015).

Inspired by the success of the Green Teens project, the Cupertino children's librarians launched a second garden for younger kids. The 600-square-foot space features several raised beds planted in large cloth bags. These include a vegetable garden; a "dino garden," complete with prehistoric-looking succulents and toy dinosaurs; a "petting zoo" filled with fuzzy, soft, and touchable plants; a scratch-and-sniff herb garden; a pole garden, topped with vines that youngsters can walk under; and a fairy garden, decorated with miniature houses. Children are encouraged to leave notes and questions for the fairies, which staff answer and post weekly. The fenced-in garden is open one hour a week on Tuesday afternoon during the spring and summer and one hour a month during fall and winter. Library staff provide self-guided activities and conduct programs on how seeds travel, how plants grow, what soil is made of, and decomposition and worms. STEM learning is reinforced through worksheets that ask the children to measure the length of leaves and describe the distinctive characteristics of each plant. Kids are urged to report the weather and what they like about the garden in a journal. They are also encouraged to draw what they observe. "Everything in the garden is meant to be handled and enjoyed by the children," library staffer Elizabeth Bartholomew explains. The entire goal of the space is to "encourage and support wonder."[5]

On the other side of the country, the Howard County Library, in Maryland, promises its users to "deliver high-quality public education for all."[6] Indeed, the Charles E. Miller Branch's Enchanted Garden was created specifically to educate, inspire a healthy lifestyle, and foster a love of nature. To achieve this, a robust roster of gardening classes and activities, for both children and adults, is offered throughout the year. Hands-on outdoor experiences occur in what is called the "demonstration garden," where children apply the everyday STEM concepts they learn inside the library. "If you take a close look at the seed heads of sunflowers or count the petals on a cucumber bloom, you, too, can discover Fibonacci's number sequence, like the children who attended our math and gardening class," says Ann Hackeling, coordinator of the Enchanted Garden (Howard County Library System 2014). An especially popular program is "What Would Peter Rabbit Eat?" during which youngsters engage in a vegetable scavenger hunt after learning about nutritious foods. The more children know about vegetables, the more likely they are to eat them, Hackeling insists. But kids aren't the only ones targeted by the branch's educational efforts; learning opportunities are offered to adults as well. The "What's in Season?" series, presented by chefs and Master Gardeners, covers topics like healthy eating, Maryland's seasonal plants, and the challenges of organic farming.

ADULT LEARNING

Gardens can be instrumental in helping adults acquire skills too. Recognizing the educational potential of gardens, the National Adult Literacy Agency, in Ireland, developed a curriculum called "Learning through Gardening," a four-module curriculum that uses universal design principles to teach basic literacy and numeracy to adults (McCormack 2014). Learners might be asked to compose a list of weeds to be pulled or write directions for planting seeds. The point is to provide learning that is fun, creative, and of interest to the learners. In this instance, adults might develop writing and computer skills by keeping a garden journal. They might also acquire an understanding of "quantity" by tallying the number of seeds sown in the garden.

Gardening can also support English language learning. Seventeen indoor aquaponic gardens have provided fodder for English language learner discussions at the Gwinnett County Public Library, in Georgia, and have even inspired intergenerational cooking programs, like "Science in the Mexican Mother's Kitchen." The mothers speak Spanish and their daughters translate as they demonstrate how to make pico de gallo and guacamole. Along the way, the group talks about Mexican cooking and then everyone eats! A similar program, "Science in the Korean Mother's Kitchen," was presented at another branch (IMLS 2018).

Finally, in California, libraries have turned traditional book discussion groups into civic engagement opportunities through an initiative called Book-to-Action, which took hold after an in-library discussion of Novella Carpenter's book *Farm City: The Education of an Urban Farmer* mobilized adult audience members to participate in a community garden workday at a local middle school (Hayward Public Library 2012). In its Book-to-Action toolkit, the California State Library pulls together socially relevant books that not only are "good reads" but might also inspire readers to do good deeds in their communities. The books are grouped by broad topic, followed by a list of potential civic engagement opportunities. For example, under the category "Sowing Seeds, Urban Farming, and Healthy Eating" are listed Janet Fletcher's *Eating Local: The Cookbook Inspired by America's Farmers*; Janisse Ray's *The Seed Underground: A Growing Revolution to Save Food*; and *Greening Cities, Growing Communities: Learning from Seattle's Urban Community Gardens* by Jeffrey Hou and colleagues—any of which might motivate readers to volunteer in the library's garden or start a seed library (Thomas 2012, 36–38).

NOTES
1. Nature Explorium, "Welcome to the Nature Explorium . . . Discover It!" www.natureexplorium.org.
2. Nature Explorium, "Programs and Activities," www.natureexplorium.org/program.html.
3. J. Delano, personal communication, January 14, 2017.
4. Several toolkits are available in English, Spanish, French, and Chinese on the C&NN website at www.childrenandnature.org/learn/toolkits.
5. E. Bartholomew, personal communication, July 25, 2017.
6. Howard County Library System, "Mission and Vision," https://hclibrary.org/about-us/mission-and-vision.

CHAPTER FOUR

Community Engagement

"The library has been the community's anchor," former Enoch Pratt Free Library director and now Librarian of Congress Carla Hayden explained when the Pennsylvania Avenue branch stayed open during a Black Lives Matter demonstration in 2015. "It's the heart of the community at good times and bad times," she said (Cottrell 2015). Indeed, libraries are the center of our communities. They are also a place to come together and discover one's self. As a child, future astrophysicist Brian Koberlein regularly visited his local library as he explored the path to his chosen career. "[I]t's hard to overstate the importance of my library," Koberlein (2018) recently related. Returning to that same library, in 2017, to speak about an upcoming solar eclipse, he knew that today's young users were hearing the same message he heard every time he walked through the door: "Welcome to the library. Here you are part of our community. Here you have standing" (Koberlein 2018).

Gardens extend the library's role even further into the community and provide a nonthreatening space to congregate. After all, "everyone has some connection to plants," Kate Chura, president of the Horticultural Society of New York (HSNY), insists. "They eat them, they see them every day" (Kuzyk 2007, 41). Gardens may provide a familiar bridge to residents who might not otherwise use the library's services. As the head of Library Environments at the University of Michigan, Emily Puckett Rodgers (2017) posits, "Great outdoor spaces provide opportunities for libraries to showcase their capacity to strengthen communities and be true placemakers—inside and out" (30). In this chapter, we look at how gardens help libraries engage their communities.

COMMUNITY CENTERS

At Oakland Public Library's César E. Chávez branch, it all began with seeds. Inspired by nearby Richmond Public Library's seed library, Chávez branch manager Peter

Villaseñor decided to start a similar program. Soon a Master Gardener asked to demonstrate container planting, and before Villaseñor knew it, a garden was growing on the library's terrace. The library's Friends group provided soil and containers, while other community members donated perennials. Many of the gardeners speak Spanish, and adult volunteers with developmental disabilities water the garden once a week. Another volunteer, from the ESL (English as a second language) class that meets in the library, comes in an hour early to help out. Caring for the garden is truly a community affair. Though local immigrants are besieged with challenges every day, the seed library and its garden are a haven and source of delight. "Their faces just light up," Villaseñor says. "It's a highlight of our library."[1]

Meanwhile, in Alamo, Texas, little did Amy Marquez know that her $100 request for an aquaponic gardening kit, on DonorsChoose.org, would turn into a communitywide project at the Marcia R. Garza Elementary School. The money funded a hydroponic tank that grows alfalfa on top and contains fish, including one named Dory, below. The garden/aquarium sits on the school library's circulation desk, attracting youngsters—and sometimes their parents—before school starts to check on the plants as well as the fish. School officials even took the tank out into the community to show people what was happening at the school. The teachers liked the idea so much that they, too, raised money, and now every classroom has its own tank. Nevertheless, students still stop by the library every day. According to Marquez, the garden makes children, who struggle with reading, feel comfortable in the library. "I just love the kids being excited as the garden's growing!" she says.[2]

Academic libraries usually take a more casual approach to gardens and community engagement. Completed in 2009, the Green Terrace, a rooftop garden connected to the library at the National Institutes of Health, provides a quiet space for library staff, visitors, and medical center patients alike. Designed using green building techniques, the 4,400-square-foot garden offers a natural, relaxing setting for individuals and groups to retreat, read, reflect, and rejuvenate. Plants include vines, native honeysuckle, sedums, and several other species that the NIH is studying for medicinal purposes. A passive cooling and rainwater management system allows the Green Terrace to also reduce the library's carbon footprint. The project won the U.S. Department of Health and Human Services' Green Champion Award for Sustainable Building Design in 2009 and the Medical Library Association's Green Project of the Year Award in 2011 (GreenRoofs.com n.d.).

GARDENING PROJECTS AND INCARCERATED PEOPLE

Gardens and their libraries can provide a lifeline connecting individuals to their communities. Nowhere is this more apparent than in prisons and jails, where gardening has been shown to reduce recidivism by 84 percent (Rosenwald 2015). Though not a formal library partner, the garden program at the Eastern Correctional Institution in Maryland relies heavily on information provided by the prison library. The Green Garden, which grows food that is donated to neighbors in Somerset County, is maintained by teams of officers and inmates. If there is an issue with planting—pumpkins have been especially challenging—an officer will dispatch a gardener to the library for research. "You just want to learn everything," says Edward Carroll, an incarcerated person who has eight books in his cell: six gardening manuals and two Bibles (Rosenwald 2015). Interestingly, Nelson Mandela also relied on library resources when he created and tended a garden during his twenty-five years in the Robben Island prison. The garden, he reportedly said, gave him a small taste of freedom (Ban Ki-Moon 2014). Indeed, Mandela took great pride in the vegetables he grew and read all the books on gardening and horticulture he found in the prison library.

In 1996, the HSNY and New York City's Departments of Correction and Education partnered to create GreenHouse, a jail-to-street program for sentenced inmates and detainees at the Rikers Island Correctional Facility (Delsesto 2013). The program integrates vocational training, environmental education, and horticultural therapy to build the skills, confidence, and motivation the participating inmates need to reenter the community at large. A key component of the program is the GreenTeam, which provides transitional employment and further training (Delsesto 2013). Today the GreenTeam maintains library gardens planted through the GreenBranches program, another HSNY initiative that creates gardens at older, more historic library outlets throughout New York City. Additional funds are used to conduct summer workshops, called "Read and Seed," for children. Besides turning the library gardens into outdoor learning centers, the workshops give GreenTeam members teaching experience. "To the credit of the public library system, the librarians and supervisors [are] accepting of the fact that the gardeners clipping hedges and teaching children how to plant tulip bulbs or harvest herbs [are] former inmates from Rikers Island," project coordinator James Jiler (2006, 150–51) relates. The GreenBranches program resulted in a 50 percent drop in the recidivism rate of Rikers' gardeners (Kuzyk 2007, 41).

FOOD GARDENS

Growing food for and with their communities is a relatively new role for libraries, but one that certainly resonates with their service mission. In Georgia, the Gwinnett County Public Library acquired a Sparks! Ignition grant, from the Institute of Museum and Library Services (IMLS), to install indoor aquaponic gardens—that is, vertical, self-contained towers that use water and minerals to feed the plants—in each of its fifteen branches. Called "Homegrown Gwinnett," the project quickly exceeded all expectations. "Gwinnett County has a lot of food deserts," the library's executive director Charles Pace explains. "There is a lack of good nutrition education and a high rate of obesity. . . . We saw these towers as educational tools aimed at all ages to solve some of these health issues the county was having" (IMLS 2018). Not only has Homegrown Gwinnett helped increase food literacy, the program has also deepened the library's roots in the community in unexpected ways. Meals on Wheels and the food subcommittee of the Gwinnett Coalition for Health and Human Services have become library partners, while everyone from teens to seniors, special education students, and new Americans have gotten involved in the project. "We haven't found an audience that hasn't been engaged with Homegrown Gwinnett and these Tower Gardens," says Barbara Spruill, director of the library's grants division (IMLS 2018). Although library staff initially targeted countywide food insecurities, they eventually uncovered other needs, including those of families and seniors living in extended-stay hotels. As a result, many of the branches now take gently used books to the hotels and food co-ops, where they also conduct off-site storytimes (IMLS 2018).

The school library media center at Portland High School, in Tennessee, has been called "the hub of the wheel" that provides cross-curricular food production and community service. The "spokes" of the project's metaphorical wheel include the school's math, science, health science, agriscience, art, food science, and special education departments. The goal of the library's garden is to provide healthy food for the pantry that serves a third of the school's students and their families. Outside agencies, such as Future Farmers of America, the state's agricultural department,

Harvesting lettuce at Gwinnett County Public Library in Georgia
Photo credit: Deborah Hakes/Georgia Public Library Service

the chamber of commerce, and Portland Cares, plus other partners, including local farmers and community volunteers, help make the program a success. Agricultural science students get service learning credit for working in the garden over the summer. Growing food in the school library media center not only provides healthy eating options, it has also forged closer connections within the school.[3]

Creating community gardens—that is, gardens maintained by groups of people—is another way libraries are cultivating food and community engagement. Participants can share responsibility for the entire garden or just work on their own plots. Established in 2010, the LibraryFarm, adjacent to the Cicero Library in Northern Onondaga, New York, offers fifty-eight individual plots for public use. Three larger collaborative gardens, tended by community members, supplied 270 pounds of produce to local food pantries in 2014. The library provides tools, land, and water, but the farm is managed via several gardening committees. Some attention has been paid to Universal Design principles, including an on-site water source and raised beds that allow ease of access and low physical effort. The LibraryFarm fosters its own community of eager learners dedicated to connecting with others while creating a shared gardening space. Participants speak of the garden's benefits, ranging from mental and physical fulfillment to charitable giving to the local food pantry. The Junior Gardeners Club constructed an "insect hotel" to capture pests, and a communal herb garden makes cooking herbs available to anyone who wants them. The LibraryFarm has been called "a unique 'makerspace' in the outdoors and a creative 'laboratory' for food literacy" (Central New York Community Foundation 2015).

The Anythink library system, outside of Denver, Colorado, offers three community gardens that use a participatory programming model. Partners include Master Gardeners and the Denver Urban Garden, but the gardens themselves are run by the community. Gardeners are encouraged to donate any produce they grow to local food banks; plus there's a big basket outside the garden gates where people can leave their excess harvest. The gardens are extremely popular, with registrations for the newest one at the Wright Farms branch filling up immediately. "I've been gardening on my own for about 30 years," Wright Farms employee Christine Gallegos relates. "I usually share what I grow with the food bank at church and family and friends, but I've never gardened with people in a community and been able to share knowledge. It's an exciting experience" (Kranz 2013).

SEED LIBRARIES, EXCHANGES, AND SWAPS

Growing food often starts with seeds and so, increasingly, libraries have begun offering seeds too. The seed library movement began in California, in 2010, and quickly spread throughout North America and beyond. Ninety such libraries were established in 2013; today they number more than 600. Libraries interested in

Seed lending library at Hall Middle School, California

Photo credit: Eliott Rogers

starting their own seed collections should consult Richmond Public Library's "Richmond Grows Seed Lending Library" webpage (Richmond Grows n.d.). Advice there includes potential partners, needed supplies, how to organize the seeds, signage for and advertising the seed library, and how to check out seeds. The process is so easy that sixth-graders can do it—and did! Students at the Hall Middle School in Larkspur, California, tested the Richmond Grows site by setting up a seed exchange in their school library. The site passed the test with flying colors, and the students' seed library continues to flourish (Landgraf 2015).

Many, but not all, seed programs are located in most types of libraries: public, academic, school, and tribal libraries.[4] Others have taken root in community centers, in cafés, and even outside a cheetah enclosure on a farm in Namibia. Despite the viability of other venues, the connection between public libraries and seed libraries seems especially obvious. As Rebecca Newburn, creator of the Richmond seed library, posits, "The public library is such a lovely fit because public libraries are about providing access, and they are a commons of the community" (quoted in Dawson 2013). Furthermore, she says, libraries store documents and so the conditions are actually really good for saving seeds (Dawson 2013). The ethos of seed libraries also fits nicely with that of many public libraries. Library users benefit from the symbiosis that supports free or inexpensive opportunities to obtain seeds and, therefore, food. Moreover, seed programs tie in with sustainability and healthy eating. When paired with gardens and garden programming, seed libraries bring communities together, increasing empowerment and diversity by attracting formerly underserved populations. The library benefits as well, connecting with residents and establishing itself as a community center in addition to serving as a source for information and recreational materials.

You may be happy to hear that seed libraries are surprisingly simple to manage. At the Harold Washington Library, in Chicago, seeds are kept in a four-drawer card catalog, sitting atop a low range of shelves in the science department. Four drawers contain seed packets. The other two house seedlings in egg cartons to demonstrate the ease of growing seeds. An instruction sheet directs users to record the seeds they borrow on an accompanying form. If borrowers have questions, they ask the librarian. There is no formal tracking system, and borrowers can opt to return the seeds or not.[5] Other libraries, however, take a more formal approach. At the Common Soil Seed Library at Omaha Public Library's Benson branch, seeds are cataloged and bar-coded. According to branch manager Rachel Steiner, the library wants to be able to deliver the packets, so community members can request specific seeds and have them sent to their local branch just like a book or any other library material. The seeds are automatically renewed to prevent them from being trapped for holds by other borrowers (Landgraf 2015).

While seed libraries request that seeds be returned, seed exchanges do not. With exchanges, borrowers take seeds but are not required to return them or even donate other seeds. Seed swaps, on the other hand, offer the unique opportunity for gardeners to exchange seeds for others not encountered in seed catalogs or stores. At the Red Hook branch of Brooklyn Public Library, native edible and nonedible seeds are displayed on a table alongside a sign that reads, "Leave some seeds, take some seeds." Handouts describe how to start a container garden, and related books are made available for checkout. Adult services librarian Michelle Montabono describes the program as a "really low effort on the part of the library."[6] The seed swap at the John Ester Tigg membership library, in Ester, Alaska, is even more "low effort." "It's a fly-by-the-seat-of-your-pants program that ends up being more a 'seed take' than seed swap," board president Syrilyn Tong explains.[7] Seeds for tomatoes, carrots, flowers, and other plants are grouped together on a table. People go into the library, which is open 24/7, browse and fill up their envelopes with the seeds they want, and then go home.

Some libraries restrict the type and provenance of the seeds they provide. The La Crosse Public Library in Wisconsin, for instance, offers only heirloom seeds—that is, "seeds that have been saved for generations by our ancestors from all parts of the world . . . [and] are open pollinated and will grow true to themselves year after year" (Hillview Urban Agriculture Center n.d.). Other sites, like the Greenfield Community College Library in Massachusetts, offer only local seeds. The goal of this particular seed library is to preserve biodiversity. "If Uncle Joe has been growing a certain variety, we'd love to be able to preserve that," project coordinator Hope Schneider says (Solomon 2017). The program returns to the roots of agriculture: seed collecting and harvesting as a communal activity.

SENSORY GARDENS

Library gardens can serve as a community hub for nongardeners too. Sensory gardens, in particular, provide space for quiet contemplation or active engagement; in other words, they are flexible enough to meet the needs of everyone in the community. Sensory gardens are inclusive because they engage all of the senses: the near senses we are most familiar with—smell, sight, hearing, taste, and touch—as well as the less well-known "far" senses—proprioception (the awareness of one's body in space) and vestibular (the sense of balance). Moreover, these types of garden offer a unique kind of accessibility for people with sensory issues, providing either a calm place to decompress for those feeling overwhelmed or strong environmental input for people experiencing a sensory deficit. Offering gardens where folks can withdraw or get energized can help lead them to homeostasis or a stable equilibrium, resulting perhaps in fewer library disruptions. Well-designed sensory gardens are especially effective for library visitors on the autism spectrum and for those with other sensory-processing disorders.[8]

Traditionally, sensory gardens were designed to stimulate all five of our near senses. A variety of colors, shapes, moving elements, contrasts, and patterns can enhance the visual experience of the garden, while plantings with intense or mild scents draw attention to different smells. Placing textured flora within arm's reach—such as planting lamb's ear in a raised bed or on a hillside or growing a tree with interesting bark next to a path—calls attention to the plants themselves and makes the garden more accessible, including to people who are blind. Herbs, fruit, and vegetables provide a wide range of taste experiences when harvested. Wind chimes, hollow logs for drums, stiff grass, and running water produce sound.

Sensory gardens can also stimulate our less familiar far senses. Proprioception is key to orienting ourselves: Am I sitting or standing, touching the floor or touching someone? The answers to these questions come from our muscles, tendons, and joints—a process that happens unconsciously. In a garden, proprioception can be engaged by providing seating and walking paths, opportunities to lift and push, and plants that offer differing levels of resistance, such as a tree limb versus a fennel frond. Our vestibular sense is regulated by the inner ear and can be stimulated by a variety of balance experiences. Different types of walking surfaces, ledges or pedestals for perching, climbing features, and various seating options not only make a garden attractive and inviting; they also provide valuable vestibular input for visitors.

The Brenda L. Papke Memorial Sensory Garden at the Staunton Public Library, in Virginia, incorporates all of these elements as well as an astonishing amount of community engagement. A model of partner collaboration, the garden is a centerpiece of the community. The library, the Talking Book Center, the city's public works and recreation and public parks departments, landscape design commissions, city engineers, and the Children's Art Network (CAN) all came together to design and build the garden, which honors Brenda L. Papke, the founder of CAN. Civic and garden clubs, a Girl Scout troop, the Downtown Development Association, and private individuals played a role in raising enough money. In addition, businesses made in-kind donations of tools and materials, plus a substantial endowment was established to fund ongoing expenses. Interns from Mary Baldwin University created Braille and audio way-finding tools to enhance accessibility, and the overall garden design was vetted by community members with disabilities. The result is a garden that fully engages visitors' senses. Many plants have strong tactile appeal, while stone walls and a fountain provide contrasting textures. The fountain also stimulates hearing. Herbs add taste and smell, and gravel paths engage proprioception as well as provide accessibility for wheelchair users. Library visitors can be found quietly reading in the garden or eating their lunches. The occasional treasure hunt draws children. The garden remains a place of wonder many years after its creation.

SPIRITUAL, CONTEMPLATIVE, AND LABYRINTH GARDENS

Spiritual gardens include some of the elements of sensory gardens but focus more on the calming and rejuvenating aspects of a designated space. The totem pole at the National Library of Medicine's garden, for instance, elicits the power of healing in a unique and spiritual way. In Ohio, a "Mary's Garden" briefly flourished at the University of Dayton's Roesch Library during spring 2017. First grown in the seventh century CE, Mary's Gardens are devotional celebrations that honor the Virgin Mary and feature plants linked to her. The Roesch exhibit was originally conceived as a way to highlight the library's collection of papers related to John S. Stokes Jr., who revived the Mary's Garden movement in the 1980s. But, as Sarah Cahalan, director of the university's Marian Library, observed, it also provided an "opportunity for everyone to think about how gardening can play a role in their lives and to reflect on the spirituality of our interactions with nature" (Filby 2017). The Roesch event had such an impact that devotees around the country were inspired to start their own Mary's Gardens, as reported by two librarians a year later (Gillingham and Harris 2018).

A fine example of a contemplative garden is Baylor University's Garden of Contentment, attached to the Armstrong Browning Library (ABL) in Waco, Texas. The garden supports the mission of the library, which holds the world's largest collection of materials related to the lives of Robert Browning and Elizabeth Barrett Browning.

Paths, chairs, and benches surround a fountain inscribed with words from Robert Browning's poem "The Guardian-Angel." As Browning and Victorian studies chair Kirstie Blair explains, "A great deal of thought went into the Garden of Contentment, and a great deal of thinking . . . happen[s] there as scholars and artists from Baylor, from Waco and from all over the world, like myself . . . visit and use this facility for inspiration in their work" (Fogleman 2012). The garden is a quiet space that provides respite from the rest of the busy campus.

A labyrinth, or wandering path, is another type of contemplative space that leads to the center of the garden and out again. For more than 4,000 years, labyrinths have had spiritual significance for humans. One of the oldest documented labyrinths was at Hawara, in ancient Egypt, and dates from the Middle Kingdom period (2040–1782 BCE). A labyrinth also decorates the Rigveda, one of the classic mandalas of Tantric literature, and dates from 1500 BCE. They were also found in ancient Celtic, Hopi, and Etruscan civilizations (Mark 2018). Wherever they appear, labyrinths are considered to be places of reflection and meditation, symbolizing change and self-discovery.

For the present-day Placitas Community Library, in New Mexico, the "winding paths" of the garden labyrinth "serve as a metaphor for our individual journeys through life—moving toward a goal and back from it" (Placitas Community Library n.d.). Adjacent to the library's several native plant gardens, the circular labyrinth was created by community members, young and old, who carried stones from home to form the path's outline. Everyone encounters the well-trodden labyrinth differently: "Adults find walking it a calming experience while children enjoy running through it" (Mountain Plains Library Association 2014–2015, 20). In Saint Paul, Minnesota, the David Barton Community Labyrinth and Reflective Garden, at Metropolitan State University, was built in memory of the library's longtime dean. The ground-level circular structure has a bench at its center and consists of a grass path defined by crushed gravel lines. It is open to the entire community, even during Minnesota's harsh winters, and is popular. People who have taken the path say that "walking the labyrinth and having the space has helped with stress, allowed for a place to meditate, and even helped with working through issues" (Pfahl and Staats 2014).

ACTIVE PLAY

At the other end of sensory experiences are gardens that encourage active play. We know from Every Child Ready to Read and other research that play supports literacy development. According to the National Literacy Trust in Great Britain, play actually lays the foundation for literacy: "Through play children learn to make and practise newer sounds. They try out new vocabulary, on their own or with friends, and exercise imagination through storytelling."[9] Children practice social skills, develop problem-solving strategies and resiliency, and create the background knowledge necessary to learn how to read. Libraries, which have always supported literacy development, are now using gardens and outdoor play areas to expand their literacy repertoire.

A walkway winds around eight distinctive play areas at Middle Country Public Library's Nature Explorium in Centereach, New York. Starting and ending at the door of the library's children's room, the sensory-friendly garden encourages all types of play, from climbing and running to pumping and splashing in water, from digging to drawing. There are even places to study, create, and build. Open seasonally, the Nature Explorium is staffed during summer daylight hours while the library is open. Library staff and partner agencies, such as the Long Island Children's Museum, conduct programs in the 5,000-square-foot garden. As one research foundation has observed, the Explorium is indeed "a place where nature and play collide and where children are firsthand witnesses to the beauty of the outdoors."[10]

Though less intricate than the Nature Explorium, Brooklyn Public Library's Park Slope garden nevertheless invites playing. Opened in 2016, the space includes a lawn, a small grass amphitheater, in-ground plantings, and raised beds, including one that is accessible to wheelchair users. Children's librarians conduct "Storyplay" programs there, which start with reading aloud and end in free play. Big Blue Blocks

Ready to garden at the Park Slope Library, Brooklyn, New York
Photo credit: Gregg Richards

Sets and other toys are made available. While the outdoor setting can be distracting, the children are less restricted and their parents tend to be more engaged in the activities than they are inside the library. Preschoolers, too, can play with manipulatives, scarves, and blocks. In this exciting open public space, one never knows what might happen next. One day, a man walking by carrying a tuba entered the garden area and played an impromptu concert for the kids![11]

NOTES

1. P. Villaseñor, personal communication, June 15, 2018.
2. A. Marquez, personal communication, October 18, 2017.
3. M. Giliam, personal communication, September 12, 2017.
4. For a list of seed libraries around the world, see Seed Libraries, "Sister Libraries," http://seedlibraries.weebly.com/sister-libraries.html.
5. Chicago Public Library, "Seed Library Project," unpaginated instruction sheet, available next to the seed library.
6. M. Montabono, personal communication, June 11, 2018.
7. S. Tong, personal communication, July 11, 2018.
8. For more information, see Biel and Peske (2018), on raising children with sensory issues; Klipper (2014), on library programming for children and teens with autism; and Etherington (2012), on sensory issues and gardens.
9. National Literacy Trust, "10 Reasons Why Play Is Important," https://literacytrust.org.uk/resources/10-reasons-why-play-important.
10. Nature Explore, "Nature Explore Classroom at Nature Explorium at Middle Country Public Library," https://certified.natureexplore.org/nature-explorium-middle-country-public-library-2.
11. C. Leckenby, E. Heath, and M. Michalek, personal communication, May 31, 2018.

CHAPTER FIVE

Library Garden Design

As youth services librarian Kimberly Alberts points out, "No matter what kind of space you have, whether you're in the middle of a downtown urban library or if you have a beautiful reading area," creating a library garden "is something you can do" (Lynch 2014, 26). Sometimes that means maximizing use of a spare piece of land or converting a parking lot into green space. In Long Beach, California, a "learning garden" was quickly pulled together when a city official noticed an empty lot next to the new Michelle Obama branch library that was about to open. He suggested that a community garden be planted in honor of the First Lady's Let's Move initiative and so, thanks to the speedy efforts of several local green organizations, the garden was built in a week, just in time for the library's grand opening (Kittrell 2017). Likewise, on Long Island, New York, the Sachem Public Library converted part of its public parking lot into a lawn plaza, called Inside/Out, featuring gardens, a ribbon walk, and space for performances and library programs. The outdoor extension is educational

Harvesting produce at Michelle Obama Neighborhood Library in Long Beach, California

Photo credit: Sheila Sorenson

as well as environmentally sensitive. "Throughout the ages libraries have served as gathering places and Inside/Out takes this concept to a new level of experience," library director Judith Willner says (Vaccaro 2010).

Both the Long Beach and Sachem libraries created opportunity where there was none before. On the other hand, when gardens are incorporated into the plans of a renovation or new building from the very beginning, they can become an integral and often dramatic part of the library's overall design. For instance, the new subterranean Green Square Library in Sydney, Australia, is designed around a one-of-a-kind sunken garden that extends through an open atrium, connecting the single-story facility to the outside world above—a "wonderful scheme," according to architect Glenn Murcutt (City of Sydney 2013). Other architects use gardens to draw community members outside the library's walls or bring nature inside. In this chapter, we look at gardens that either

- were built as a general feature of the library's architecture,
- provide a central theme to an outdoor reading area,
- help define or redefine the library's role, or
- serve as an anchor element of a "green design."

ARCHITECTURAL FEATURES

The Leslie F. Malpass Library at the University of Western Illinois epitomizes the idea of a garden as architectural feature. Planters surround the library's central stairwell and a solarium, called the Garden Lounge, serves as a program area. Just a brief peak at the library's promotional YouTube video reveals plants strategically placed everywhere![1] Indeed, at one point, Malpass was home to some 2,000 plants. "The library was designed to have a garden throughout the building," dean of libraries Michael Lorenzen explains.[2] Staff and students alike love it. Calling the library "beautiful, sort of an inside-out structure," one staff member says she never feels like she's in a building. "There's no real border between inside and outside."[3] Another staff member describes the library as "a rain forest."[4] "I love the library's beauty," a graduate student remarks. "It's a beautiful space."[5]

The Reno branch of the Washoe County Library was also designed around an interior garden, stretching several stories above the ground floor. When plans to build the library next to the Truckee River fell through, the architect reportedly said, "If we can't put the library in the park, we'll put a park in the library," resulting in one of the most magnificent library interiors in the country (Robison 2014). The branch is, in fact, so impressive that, in the early 1970s, city officials in Huntington Beach, California, recommended that their world-famous architects, Richard and Dion Neutra, replicate it for their new central library. "The library board had seen a library in Nevada which had a great deal of greenery inside the building, and they thought this would be a wonderful environment to read and study by," Dion Neutra

(1998) related many years later. The Neutras agreed. Bringing the outside into the Huntington Beach library became "a very key element" of its architectural design (Epting 2015).

"Architecture is about restoring man to his historic relationship to nature and its various elements," Richard Neutra was fond of saying (quoted in Stockteam n.d.). At the Huntington Beach library an atrium rises from the ground floor, as plants and water surround a central, open-air stacks area. "With all of its lush foliage, the interior itself almost feels park-like," one recent visitor enthused (Lindsay 2017). Readers are encouraged to walk among trees and flowers to find a place to sit, as large pillars topped with circular fountains reach upward. "Inside there is the outside," an early reviewer observed (City of Huntington Beach, Information Office 1975, 48). Another describes the library's interior as making "you feel at home." The end result, the reviewer goes on to say, "is the friendliest, most handsome public building we've ever seen" (Buffum 1975).

Equally welcoming is the Winter Garden in Chicago, located on the top floor of the Harold Washington Library Center. Called one of the area's greatest secret gardens, the glass-domed atrium occupies most of the central library's ninth floor and is a lovely reminder of Chicago's motto *Urbs in horto* or "City in a Garden" (LaTrace 2015). Natural light floods the area year-round as trees in containers dot the center of the room. Ivy, planted in marble boxes around the room's perimeter, is attached to special panels, giving the impression of a demi-green wall. Although designed primarily as an ornamental reading room, this space is frequently used as a supplemental auditorium, hosting programs, staff training, and special events.

Indoor garden at Huntington Beach Public Library, California

Photo credit: Copyright image courtesy of Huntington Beach Public Library

READING GARDENS

A reading garden is an outdoor extension of an indoor space, where visitors can relax and read. Gardening expert Amy Grant (2018) suggests several factors to consider when creating a reading garden:

- **Location:** Does the site provide an impressive vista or view of the entire garden? Salt Lake City Public Library's rooftop garden, for instance, is renowned for its breathtaking views of the Wasatch Mountains.
- **Shade versus sunshine:** While people reading paper books may appreciate natural sunlight, e-book readers will no doubt prefer shade.
- **Tranquility:** Is the garden located in a quiet spot or next to a busy street? If the purpose is to provide a comfortable space where visitors can relax and read, then the quieter the better.
- **Audience:** If the garden is intended for children, then water features and toxic plants should be avoided. In addition, paths should be sufficiently smooth and wide enough to accommodate wheelchairs as well as baby carriages.
- **Seating:** Chairs and benches should be plentiful and encourage contemplative moments. Tables for using laptops or even eating lunch should also be made available.

Reading gardens can be grandiose, Grant (2018) says, or as uncomplicated as a bench placed amid a bed of roses. In Santiago, Chile, the Biblioteca Nacional has an outdoor reading area large enough to feature a train car that houses popular works of fiction (Chileapart.com, 2014). Elsewhere, in Honolulu, the Mānoa Elementary School library has a simple outdoor reading room thanks to the creative thinking of its librarian, Imelda Amano.[6] Noticing that several teachers were starting to cultivate classroom gardens, she decided the library should have one, too, and so researched reading gardens. Within two months, the area fronting the library was cleared, weeded, and tilled, allowing the Library Club to plant flowers and herb donations. The garden looks out onto a cherry blossom tree and the majestic mountains of Oahu.

Another less formal reading garden was started by Shawn Friend-Begin, librarian at the Rheinland-Pfalz Library located on the Landstuhl Regional Medical Center Army post in Germany. Realizing that "military families, who typically move every few years, don't often have a garden of their own or are even familiar with flowers," Friend-Begin decided to create a space filled with flowers and herbs.[7] Between the comfortable seating and the Wi-Fi, the garden is a popular spot for reading. "An appreciation of, and need for, a beautiful environment is severely underrated," Friend-Begin notes.[8]

Much more formal, yet just as enticing, is the Dudley reading garden, located behind a wrought-iron gate adjacent to the Lamont Library on the Harvard campus. The space, which is lush with native plants and ivy, is open to students, faculty, and library staff April through October. Named after Thomas Dudley, a founder of both Harvard and the city of Cambridge, the garden was created in 1999 to help celebrate the library's fiftieth anniversary. It's been called a "secret garden" and "little-known treasure" that offers a serene refuge from "the stress of . . . Harvard" and "the turbulence of the world beyond" (Saiger 2017). Visitors can either relax on classical semicircular concrete benches or wander along a path through the thick foliage. All are invited into "the peace and tranquility of the garden, where time is measured in shadows" (Andrewes 2014).

Much like the rooftop spaces of the early twentieth century, many of today's reading gardens are once again located atop library buildings. The new central library in Austin, Texas, is not only landscaped in an outstanding display of full-grown native plants; it also provides a rooftop reading room that doubles as a rentable event space overlooking the city and Lady Bird Lake. Yuccas, flowering perennials, and grasses flow across a mounded central planting bed, surrounded by seating under an L-shaped arbor covered in solar panels. Plus there's an oak tree, visible from inside the library. The roof garden is "one of the big attractors of the building," explains biophilia consultant Kathy Zarsky in a talk on the library's sustainability. "It is one of the first places people go" (Office of Sustainability, City of Austin 2018). "I love this space," enthuses garden blogger Pam Penick (2017) about the rooftop reading room. "[It's] one of the coolest spaces in the library."

Opened in 2003, Salt Lake City's central library has a rooftop garden that provides a quiet place of contemplation as well as a stunning 360-degree view of the city and surrounding valley. Former executive director Nancy Tessman once compared the library and its garden to "an open mind" that "look[s] outward in every direction" (Berry 2006, 32). Accessed via glass elevators and a "walkable wall" that starts at ground level and climbs five stories, the garden has been called "beloved" and "one of the gems of Salt Lake City" (Scott 2018; Safdie Architects 2003). Moshe Safdie, the world-famous architect who designed Salt Lake City's central library, also designed the central library in Vancouver, which recently opened its rooftop reading area. Originally planned to be a public area, the garden remained off-limits when the library opened in 1995 and instead became "one of Vancouver's most high-profile hidden spaces" (Donaldson 2017). More than twenty years later, the roof has been reenvisioned as an outdoor extension of the library (Chan 2018; "Vancouver Public Library Rooftop Garden" 2010). The 8,000-square-foot garden is designed primarily for informal use. As library director Sandra Singh explains, "People can just come up with their coffee and get a brief respite from the bustle of downtown" (Donaldson 2017). The renovation took over a year to complete and included pumping soil, through a hose, to the top of the building to create the garden. "It was a massive transformation involving taking out half of the ninth floor and turning that into the rooftop garden," library official Carol Nelson explained (Seucharan 2018). The space is planted with trees, grasses, and flowering arbutus (Donaldson 2017).

REDEFINING LIBRARY ROLES

"Outdoor spaces can combine natural and built elements that draw people to the site, encourage them to connect with each other, and provide a variety of functions," one library expert writes (Rodgers 2017, 30). Indeed, in the late nineteenth and early twentieth centuries, the library's landscape was often as important as the building itself. When city leaders began planning the Albright Memorial Library in Scranton, Pennsylvania, in 1890, they hired none other than Frederick Law Olmsted, the famous landscape architect responsible for Central Park in New York City (NYC), to design the library's grounds. Only the best gardens could complement a library built to resemble a fifteenth-century French chateau made of Indiana limestone (Rybezynski 2001).

Garden design was also a big part of the new Los Angeles central library that opened in 1926. The west entrance, in particular, was "bordered by wide shallow steps and framed by cypress trees, a procession of three reflecting pools . . . imbued with a sense of ceremonial dignity" (Los Angeles Public Library n.d.). The pools, called "The Well of the Scribes," featured a bronze relief that celebrated writers and literature worldwide. Architect Bertram Goodhue's plan was to continue "the experience of intellectual immersion" beyond the central library's walls (Orlean 2018, 190). The entire ambience was so stimulating that the gardens merited a mention in the Works Progress Administration's guide to the "City of Angels" in 1939 (Federal Writers Project 2011, 158).

A stellar example of a present-day landscape that complements its library's design is the Southfield Public Library, which received the Keep Michigan Beautiful award in 2005.[9] Designed in conjunction with the new library, the surrounding greenery helps soften the modern-styled three-story building made of brick and glass. The Imaginarium Garden, located in the Children's Terrace, is especially lively with its metal butterfly bench, rubberized reading circle, and a spectacular twenty-foot flying sculpture of the book *The Secret Garden*. In addition, the courtyard features plenty of flora, including maple trees, Canadian serviceberry, gingko, blue fescue, and dwarf fountain grass (Kelly n.d.). Although the Imaginarium is "architectural on the outside," architect Paul Andriese explains, the interior is meant "to foster a sense of discovery . . . with notches and nooks and crannies for kids to explore" (Kelly n.d.).

While many libraries, like Southfield, Salt Lake City, and Huntington Beach, incorporated foliage into their designs from the very beginning, other libraries don't think about gardens until they undergo a renovation or landscaping update. Instigated by the Horticultural Society of New York in 1997, the GreenBranches initiative strives to plant gardens at older, more historic library outlets throughout New York City's five boroughs. Brooklyn's Saratoga branch was the first to benefit. The Woodhaven branch, in Queens, and the Arlington branch soon followed ("In Brooklyn, a Garden" 1997). Other branches participating throughout the city include Flatbush, Brownsville,

Brooklyn Heights, and Red Hook (Kuzyk 2007). The Queens Library at Whitestone added a water garden, a trellis for shade, a planter wall, and seasonal low-maintenance plantings through the GreenBranches program. A trellis was also installed at Brooklyn's Stone Avenue garden, which now boasts a quilt-like arrangement of planter beds to accommodate gardeners of all ages and abilities (Marpillero Pollak Architects n.d.). In Park Slope, the 1906 Carnegie library now has a 3,700-square-foot green space that features a reading circle, storytelling garden, benches, a drinking fountain, and amphitheater. "The garden is an important resource for the community, as it promotes healthy living and serves as an area for neighbors to gather in a place connected with learning and community," a commissioner of the NYC department of design and construction said (Leibel 2017).

In 2014, the Sun Ray branch of the Saint Paul Public Library, in Minnesota, completely transformed itself into a place where families can engage with nature. Library manager Rebecca Ryan admits she wasn't sure her community members would respond well to nature programs; but when the remodeled library opened with an outdoor pollinator garden, many people began to express interest. The garden helped establish Sun Ray's new role as a "nature-smart" library (Otto 2016). The effect has been especially profound on younger users, who engage with the garden and participate in outdoor activities offered by the library. "Books nurture learning and inner imagination, while play in nature engages the sense of curiosity and exploration critical to healthy brain development," library partner and C&NN cofounder Richard Louv posits. "Putting both these essential childhood experiences in one place . . . effects . . . whole neighborhoods" (Children & Nature Network 2015). Ryan concurs, citing evidence that the library "is connecting young people and families to the outdoors in a really unique way by pairing the imagination of reading with exploration in nature" (Friends of the Saint Paul Public Library 2016). For its efforts, the Sun Ray branch won an Environmental Initiative Award in 2016 (Friends of the Saint Paul Public Library 2016).

Meanwhile, back in Scranton, the once-proud Olmsted garden, which was replaced by a parking lot in the 1950s, was happily re-created when the original landscaping plans were rediscovered during the library's centenary in 1992. The Albright Memorial Library is now once again surrounded by thirty-one species of trees, deciduous bushes, evergreen shrubs, and perennials. "Hardly the Sheep Meadow of Central Park," Olmsted's biographer Witold Rybezynski (2001) admits, "but a pleasing choreography of greens" nonetheless.

Los Angeles central library's gardens have also been revitalized and are now considered one of the city's "most beautiful downtown spaces" ("Maguire Gardens" 2012). Desperate for a parking lot, staff suggested paving the library's West Lawn gardens in 1969. Debate over the proposal was so heated that southern California architect Robert Alexander chained himself to a rock in protest, but staff prevailed (Orlean 2018, 236–37). The once glorious West Lawn was bulldozed to become a parking lot. However, when the central library was nearly destroyed by fire in 1986 (Soter 1993, 76), famed landscape architect Lawrence Halpren was hired to design the now renamed Maguire Gardens as part of the building's reconstruction. The small but well-used park-like space currently offers plenty of trees, lawns, seating, and several fountains. But, by far, the most notable feature is a three-tiered series of pools and steps, called "Spine," that lead to the library's west entrance. Mimicking the former West Lawn's "Well of the Scribes," sculptor Jud Fine decorated the pools with print alphabets and other iconography that evoke the library's purpose. "Like a book, the site can be read," Fine explains. "The step risers, with their text composition, are like pages" (Fine and Reese 1993, 13). His work, though, is more than just an art installation. "The subject and the greater entity of 'Spine' is the library," Fine insists (Central Docents 2016).

GREEN BUILDINGS AND LEED CERTIFICATION

The terms *green*, *sustainable*, and *environmentally friendly* tend to be used interchangeably to refer to practices that minimize the potentially harmful effects of construction on the environment and health, as environmental considerations have become an increasingly important part of architectural design. According to the U.S. Green Building Council, a green building is one that incorporates the following design elements:

- Sustainable site selection and development
- Water conservation
- Energy efficiency
- Local and environmentally neutral resources, materials conservation, and waste reduction
- Quality indoor environment
- Ease and efficiency of operational and maintenance practices[10]

LEED (Leadership in Energy and Environmental Design) certification is the standard for ranking green buildings. Points, awarded for architectural features that make a facility sustainable, can result in certification on one of four levels: certified, silver, gold, or platinum. Since gardens address several of the green building criteria, they often help libraries achieve LEED certification.

Although his work predates current-day LEED mandates, architect Frank Lloyd Wright is well known for his integration of sites and buildings. His design for the Marin County Civic Center (MCCC), in Northern California, epitomizes this concept. The entire complex, which houses a county administrative wing, the Anne T. Kent California History Room, an archival collection, and MCCC branch library, blends seamlessly with the surrounding landscape. Atriums, which run along the center of each building, provide "employees and visitors with the pleasing prospect of either looking inward to the planted, sky-lit malls or outward to green trees and hills" (County of Marin n.d.). Wright's use of natural light and topography to reduce the impact of the building and its footprint illustrates the importance of site selection and garden placement. Wright's buildings are considered sustainable because he maximized the use of existing natural design features. Today's architects might also choose to add elements that improve some part of the existing site. For instance, introducing features that reduce the "heat-island effect"—that is, the radiant heat caused by urban surfaces—or minimize rainwater runoff. Incorporating environmentally friendly elements, such as rain gardens or green walls and roofs, contributes to increased points toward LEED certification for site selection.

Many libraries use gardens as part of their water management and drainage systems. Rain gardens absorb and filter rainwater, reducing runoff into storm drains and curtailing watershed pollution. These types of gardens can also help reduce localized flooding. The Rosemary Garfoot Public Library, which claims to be Wisconsin's first green library, planted a rain garden outside its main entrance. Staff estimate that the garden allows 30 percent more water to soak into the ground than conventional lawns. The library was awarded silver-level LEED certification and four out of five points for water management (Rosemary Garfoot Public Library 2007). Gardens alongside the East Boston branch of Boston Public Library also help manage storm water runoff and contributed to gold-level LEED certification when the library opened in 2013. The building's roof includes a rain catchment system that drains into the garden and eventually into underground tanks instead of through the city's storm drains. High-efficiency irrigation controllers are also used. As a result, the library has realized a 70 percent reduction in potable water use (Green Engineer 2017).

Water and waste management can also be achieved through rooftop gardens. Though not LEED-certified, the J. Willard Marriott Library at the University of Utah, in Salt Lake City, has a rooftop garden that channels rainwater but is not open to the public. Instead, the roof, which is covered in local drought-resistant plants, provides a protective membrane over the library's automated retrieval center. Three measuring devices, called lysimeters, determine changes in soil due to loss of moisture. By collecting these data, the university hopes to explore green roof choices and identify what works best in the local climate. The study is also evaluating how the green roof impacts the library's energy consumption.[11]

Rooftop gardens not only help with water management, they can also improve energy efficiency throughout the building. In Singapore, the National Library uses bioclimatic landscaping, sky terraces, and roof gardens to lower ambient temperature (National Library Board 2018). In Illinois, a garden covers about 30 percent of the Addison Public Library's roof, thus reducing heat-island effect as well as energy use. The green roof also provides acoustic insulation and improved air quality (Jordan 2013, 103; Central Minnesota Libraries Exchange n.d.). The central library in

Madison, Wisconsin, is also insulated by a rooftop garden, as is the Sam J. Racadio Library and Environmental Learning Center in Highland, California. Both of these libraries are gold-level LEED certified (Anest 2018; Madison Public Library n.d.).

Living walls, or "vertical gardens," also help with energy efficiency. Like rooftop gardens, external living walls reduce urban heat-island effect by absorbing sunlight through plant respiration. They also provide wildlife refuge and deter graffiti. The Semiahmoo Public Library in Ontario, Canada, has the largest vertical garden in North America, with over 10,000 plants covering 3,000 square feet of wall. Described by one reporter as a "veritable forest," this amazing garden produces crops, such as lettuce and peppers, while also serving as a habitat to bees, butterflies, and hummingbirds (Laylin 2011). An exterior living wall is also a key element of the recently renovated Brighton branch, Boston Public Library's first LEED-certified building.[12]

Interior vertical gardens are equally beneficial to the environment (Dalglish 2018). Not only do they add a dramatic architectural feature to any room, but the microorganisms that live on the plants' roots purify the air by consuming noxious gasses, such as benzene and formaldehyde. Living walls may even produce oxygen and serve as a fire retardant. Plus they help recycle rainwater, creating pure water for plants and gray water for use in other parts of the building. The water's constant movement through the plants creates a soothing ambient sound that helps mitigate noise.

Two academic libraries in Canada provide excellent examples of interior vertical gardens. The recently renovated R. Howard Webster Library, at Concordia University in Montreal, has nine living walls filled with "philodendron 'lemon lime,' pothos 'neon' and pothos 'marble'" plants, chosen for their tolerance to various elements (Webster Library 2017). Toronto's Centennial College Library and Academic Facility, on the other hand, features a single four-story vertical garden on one end of its multifloor atrium. The garden is integrated into an air filtration system that removes 80 percent of airborne contaminants, including off-gassing from building materials and computer equipment. The system, which was originally developed for use in space stations, requires far less outdoor intake than traditional buildings, resulting in lower energy costs (Bernard 2012). "That wall is not just pretty plants," lead architect Donald Schmitt says. "It's an integral part of the building's air circulation system. It keeps the air fresh" (Dalglish 2018). Not a surprise that Centennial's library is gold-level LEED certified.

Another example is the Harvard Graduate School of Education's Gutman Library, which installed four interior living walls during its 2010 renovation. The vertical gardens are welcoming as well as environmentally healthy. "The walls have attracted a great deal of attention. People touch them to confirm that they are real, living plants," library director John W. Collins enthuses. "They add an air of freshness, a sense of warmth and coziness, and, despite their location in a busy area of the library, they exude tranquility and seem to lower stress levels" (Harvard Library

2012). The renovated Gutman Library was awarded LEED's highest ranking, platinum certification.

NOTES
1. Kyleh488, "Malpass Library—WIUTV3," YouTube, published February 17, 2010, www.youtube.com/watch?v=DqOU1GnTtOU.
2. M. Lorenzen, personal communication, December 8, 2016.
3. K. Nichols, personal communication, May 16, 2018.
4. M. Cameron, personal communication, May 16, 2018.
5. U. Igwa, personal communication, May 16, 2018.
6. I. Amano, personal communication, December 12, 2016.
7. S. Friend-Begin, personal communication, April 4, 2017.
8. S. Friend-Begin, personal communication, April 5, 2017.
9. Keep Michigan Beautiful, "Southfield Public Library," www.keepmichiganbeautiful.org/awards/sfpl.html.
10. Adapted from U.S. General Services Administration, "Sustainable Design," GSA.gov, www.gsa.gov/real-estate/design-construction/design-excellence/sustainability/sustainable-design.
11. J. Willard Marriott Library, "Green Roof Lysimeters," www.lib.utah.edu/info/green/rooftop-garden.php.
12. Johnson Roberts Associates, "Boston Public Library, Brighton Branch," http://johnson-roberts.com/brighton-branch-library.

CHAPTER SIX

Planning and Managing the Library Garden

Throughout this book we have shown the benefits of numerous real-life gardening projects, from Ronald, the child with autism, who pointed to the color purple for the first time in a Brooklyn Public Library garden to the staff member who regularly visits the National Library of Medicine's herb garden because it reminds her of home half a world away. Gardens, like any library program, provide their own unique set of joys. But they can also present problems. As former public library director Mary Wilkins Jordan (2013) warns, challenges can range anywhere from the mundane—"weeds, weeds, weeds"—to the more complicated—a leaky rooftop garden (107–9). "The challenges involved in continued operation of a library garden should be considered prior to starting in on this project," Jordan reminds us, "but should not dissuade libraries from considering a garden of their own" (104).

PLANNING THE GARDEN

Many libraries may think that "if we build it, they will come"—after all, who doesn't enjoy a beautiful garden? But like other successful library programs, a garden requires lots of planning. "Determine the primary purpose of the garden, location, initial cost, ongoing cost . . . and design," a staff member from the Addison Public Library, in Illinois, suggests. "Research carefully, talk to libraries that have initiated some kind of garden, and plan for its use" (Jordan 2013, 107). Planning allows administrators to make informed decisions before offering a program that may end up having a profound impact on the library's services. Alicia Doktor, manager of the Colonial Heights branch of Sacramento Public Library, advises creating a five-year garden plan to avoid being distracted by the "next shiny thing."[1] A well-conceived plan provides a road map to help the library stay on course.

In planning a library garden, managers should ask themselves several questions before proceeding with the project:

- **What is the purpose of the garden?** Is it meant to provide community engagement or are the plants merely ornamental? The Glencarlyn Library's garden, in Virginia, actually has its own mission statement, promising to "provide resources for Arlington residents to learn how to create gardens in both the suburban and urban landscape."[2]
- **How will the garden help the library achieve its mission?** In Washington State, the Olympia Timberland Library agreed to work with the nonprofit organization GRuB (Garden-Raised Bounty) to create a demonstration garden that clearly supports two of the library's service priorities: "promote the library as a community gathering place" and "strengthen resources, services, and events that promote community interaction" (Feddern n.d.).
- **Who will maintain the garden? The library? The city's gardening crew? The Friends group or local garden club?** Many library gardens are cared for by Master Gardeners or volunteer gardening clubs. Other libraries delegate responsibility to staff.
- **Where should the garden be located? Adjacent to the library? On the roof? Inside the library?** Should part of the public parking lot be converted into a garden? How will the garden be configured? Most of these issues are discussed in chapter 5 on library garden design.
- **What types of plants should the library grow?** Should the library feature native flora or concentrate on vegetable- and fruit-bearing plants? Which flowers will best attract pollinators? And what about ornamental plants? Do they serve a purpose or are they just an extravagance? The "growing zone" in which the library is located may dictate some of these decisions, but staff will also want to consult with a gardening expert.
- **How can the library guarantee accessibility to people of all ages and abilities?** What types of paths best accommodate wheelchairs and strollers? Which plants best stimulate one's senses? What are the best planting bed dimensions? In Palos Verdes, California, the library built two wood planter boxes on the asphalt at the back of its parking lot. Cindy observed a group of veterans taking a particular interest in the project because they could easily move their wheelchairs from one box to the next.
- **Which resources are needed to support the garden?** Is there a toolshed nearby? And what about water? The Zion-Benton Public Library, in Illinois, discovered that its main water spigot was on the other side of the building only after they planted their garden (Jordan 2013, 107). Access to water is especially critical in regions that regularly undergo drought.
- **What permissions are needed to create a public garden?** When the Chula Vista Public Library, in California, decided to make its parking lot more environmentally friendly by planting drought-tolerant gardens throughout, staff had to get permission from the public works department to reduce the number of parking spaces.[3] Other jurisdictions may have to adhere to land use laws.

- **How can funding be gained and sustained? And what is the role of volunteers and partner organizations?** Many, if not most, library gardens are funded initially through donations or a grant. These issues are discussed in chapter 7.
- **How will the benefits of the garden be measured?** The importance of evaluating garden programs and how to do it are addressed in chapter 8.

MANAGING MAINTENANCE

"The care and feeding of a living system is not for everybody. You have to be the right person," a staff member recently observed about her library's garden. "You need a daily eye."[4] Indeed, while administrators and outside groups might enthuse over the benefits of creating a library garden, deciding who should maintain that garden is another matter altogether. Some jurisdictions have maintenance crews that care for outdoor spaces as part of their regular routine. But as one official said, in the past "[we] had real gardeners, [and today] we have a kid with headphones and a hedge clipper" (Rybezynski 2001). Therefore, green-thumb staff members may be enlisted to help tend their libraries' gardens. The city of Mill Valley, California, for instance, maintains the grounds surrounding the library, but the library is responsible for the upkeep of its demonstration garden.[5] Likewise, in Chula Vista, the city manages the parking lot, but the library has to care for the native flora recently planted there.[6]

Volunteers and partner agencies can be a welcome boon when caring for a library garden. However, as one anonymous staff member says, amateur gardeners can be inconsistent and may even do more harm than good. So some libraries hire a professional gardener to care for their plants. At the Washoe County Library, the same person has watered and pruned the indoor atrium every week since the Reno branch opened in the mid-1960s.[7] In Sacramento, the Rancho Cordova branch pays an agricultural service, called the Yisrael Family Farm, to tend the library's vegetable garden and conduct green programs for local youth. "Urban farming is not just for food production," family head Chanowk Yisrael says. "It's a community-building tool." According to the Yisrael Family's motto, they're hoping to transform "the hood for good" (Cummins 2017).

SHARING RESPONSIBILITY AND COSTS

For some jurisdictions, offering a community garden where residents can grow food for themselves and others is a natural extension of the library's mission. In South Sioux City, Nebraska, starting a garden "was a practical addition to the library's traditional services, as many area residents are blue-collar workers who live in food deserts," library director David Mixdorf explains (Inklebarger 2016). Today the library offers two community gardens—one at a school and the other at a church—with a special emphasis on serving Hispanic market gardeners. Participants pay from $10 to $25 a year to rent a plot, depending on the size of the individual space (Inklebarger 2016; Thomas 2011). Other libraries also charge a fee to participate in their community gardens. Anythink gardeners pay $35 a year to rent ten-foot-square plots on the library's property (Kranz 2013). And while the Westbank Libraries, in Texas, no longer charge an annual fee, they do require either a $50 or $100 deposit, which is refunded only after the plot is completely vacated (Meyers 2017). All rental fees go toward defraying the cost of the gardens, including providing water and tools. Gardeners apply for library plots but are often faced with a long waiting list.

Most, if not all, libraries have written rules for using their community gardens. They may also require gardeners to sign and submit a liability release. Some of these forms are posted online, but others must be picked up at the sponsoring library. The LibraryFarm (2017), in Cicero, New York, and the Westbank Libraries (2018), provide excellent examples of library garden rules and gardener "agreements." (For the complete documents, see appendix B.) When deciding whether to start a community garden, libraries should consider the following:

- **Length of growing season:** Though not an issue in states like California, where plants grow all year round, other environments are definitely impacted by the seasons, which may limit when the gardens are available to use. At the LibraryFarm, gardeners must register by March 15 to participate. All beds must be tilled by June 1 and planted by June 15. Gardens are active until November 1.
- **Hours of operation:** Westbank gardeners are given an access code to the garden gate and toolshed and so are able to use the facilities at any time. At the LibraryFarm, however, users must check out the key to the toolshed from the library circulation desk and so their hours are more limited.
- **Use of organic materials:** Gardeners at both Westbank and the LibraryFarm are required to use organic gardening methods only. No artificial herbicides, insecticides, fungicides, or chemical fertilizers are permitted.
- **Plant restrictions:** Westbank gardeners are allowed to grow plants up the property's fence, as long as the plants don't grow horizontally beyond the plot boundary. On the other hand, LibraryFarm gardeners may not grow plants higher than four feet or in a manner that blocks the sun or rain from a neighbor's plot. Invasive and insidious plants, as well as most perennials, are not allowed.
- **How to handle weeds:** Gardeners are responsible for keeping their plots weed-free at both libraries. A weed whacker is available at Westbank. Gardeners are advised to wear long pants and eye protection when whacking weeds. The garden composter should not be used when discarding weeds and diseased plants.

Many gardeners enjoy participating in the library's community garden. As Anythink public services director Ronnie Storey-Ewoldt says, "With gardens and the libraries, it's about making a connection with the community" (Kranz 2013). The Library-Farm has its own Facebook page.[8] At Westbank, the community garden coordinator communicates with the gardeners via a monthly e-newsletter and private e-mail discussion list. The library also holds "Garden Get-Together" potlucks twice a year on weekend afternoons.

PERMISSIONS AND LEGAL CONSIDERATIONS

One of the first things library staff should research, of course, is whether they are even allowed to create a garden on their property. Local governments use zoning to designate permitted land use based on mapped zones that separate incompatible land uses from one another. Zoning or planning codes and ordinances determine which activities can and cannot occur in each land use zone. The broadest categories of land use are

- agricultural,
- residential,
- commercial,
- industrial,
- public,
- mixed use, and
- open space.

Agricultural activities are usually restricted to industrial zones and, to a lesser degree, commercial zones, where free distribution of produce may also be allowed. Administrators should check the city's general plan to identify in which land use zone the library is located (Chamberlin, Eskandari-Qajar, and Orsi n.d.).

Staff will also want to look into nuisance laws prohibiting activities that interfere with a neighbor's "comfortable enjoyment of life or property." For instance, blight ordinances are used to challenge front yard gardens in some areas. Because land use laws vary from jurisdiction to jurisdiction, it is always best to contact the local building department to determine what exactly is and is not allowed (Chamberlin, Eskandari-Qajar, and Orsi n.d.). Building codes should also be consulted when considering the addition of permanent structures, like a greenhouse or garden gazebo.

Libraries hoping to start a community food garden will want to ensure that certain crops aren't prohibited due to potential pest infestation. For example, in the early 1990s, the provincial government of Prince Edward Island, Canada, banned the growing of potatoes to prevent the spread of potato blight through gardens. More recently, Texas temporarily banned the sale of citrus plants to prevent the spread of Asian citrus psyllid, known to cause citrus greening disease. State extension agencies, Master Gardeners, and local botanical gardens are good sources for this type of information.

Seed libraries have their own sets of rules and are governed by state agricultural laws. Guidelines on seed exchanges and libraries differ from place to place. In 2016, the American Association of Seed Control Officials amended the Recommended Uniform State Seed Law (RUSSL) to "exempt seed libraries and other non-commercial seed sharing initiatives" (Association of American Seed Control Officials 2016). The good news is that many states have changed their laws to allow libraries and other noncommercial entities to offer seed libraries and exchanges, though some, like Nebraska, have not. In states where these activities are legal, the key is to host a program, under a noncommercial use exemption, that does not require seed return. To comply with the law, seed libraries can *encourage* return but cannot require or enforce it—otherwise the program would become a commercial enterprise and, therefore, would be forbidden. For more information, libraries should check with legal counsel or their state's department of agriculture.

ACCESSIBILITY

Since 1990 and the enactment of the Americans with Disabilities Act (ADA), all U.S. government agencies, places of public accommodation, and entities receiving federal funds are required to be fully accessible to people with disabilities. To make buildings accessible, architects and others use Universal Design principles to meet the needs of current and future users. These are the seven basic principles of Universal Design:

1. **Equitable use:** is useful and marketable to people with diverse abilities
2. **Flexibility in use:** accommodates a wide range of individual needs and abilities
3. **Simple and intuitive use:** easy to understand, regardless of the user's experience, knowledge, language skills, or current concentration level
4. **Perceptible information:** communicates necessary information effectively to the user, regardless of ambient conditions or the user's sensory abilities
5. **Tolerance for error:** minimizes hazards and adverse consequences of accidental or unintended actions
6. **Low physical effort:** can be used efficiently and comfortably and with a minimum of fatigue
7. **Size and space for approach and use:** appropriate size and space provided for approach, reach, manipulation, and use, regardless of user's body size, posture, or mobility[9]

This framework should guide us as we make library gardens, as well as libraries, into fully accessible and welcoming spaces. *Equitable use* can be addressed by placing garden beds at various heights, from ground level to thirty-six inches. Using

Accessible gardening at Brooklyn Public Library's Red Hook branch
Photo credit: Gregg Richards

trellises, planting walls, benches attached to planting beds, window boxes, columnar plants, and espalier-trained shrubs helps achieve a wide range of accessibility. On the other hand, *flexible use* and *low physical effort* can be achieved through movable beds, a variety of tool grips, and telescoping tools that can be used by both right- and left-handed people. The original Inclusive Services garden at Brooklyn Public Library featured a section of movable beds that had mesh netting through which plants could grow. One child, who came to the program on a stretcher in an ambulance, was able to garden with his peers because the movable planter box could be placed on a table near him.

The principle of *simple and intuitive use* invites everyone to use the garden, despite little knowledge about plants or gardening. Uncluttered planting and visual clues, such as pictogram signs, enable minimal explanation and supervision. In addition, clear, unambiguous instructions, warnings, and other facts, presented in simple, linear sentences using a serif-free font, enhance *perceptible information*. *Tolerance for error* avoids potential frustrations and creates a warm and supportive environment. Library gardens should be the antithesis of traditional classrooms, where learners are sometimes chastised and punished for their mistakes. To make the garden as trauma-free as possible, staff should use only plants that can be easily replaced, in case visitors accidentally weed or step on them. Finally, *low physical effort* and appropriate *size and space for approach and use* can easily be achieved through a good design that includes ADA-compliant rises, ramps, and adequate spatial dimensions. Paths should be conducive to both walking and rolling and mulch and loose gravel should be avoided. Tight spaces should also be avoided, if at all possible. If not, then plants should be grown vertically to free up what might be an otherwise difficult spot to navigate (Kavanagh et al. n.d.).

WHAT TO GROW AND HOW TO GROW IT

Gardening is the act of cultivating plants in an appropriate environment so the plants will thrive and produce flowers, foliage, root or leaf vegetables, and fruits or herbs. Gardening differs from farming in that gardening is considered by many to be a hobby and a relaxing activity. Types of gardens include

- **indoor**—plants grown inside a residence, conservatory, or greenhouse;
- **native plants**—a garden in harmony with its surroundings;
- **water**—plants adapted to pools and ponds or grown hydroponically in an aquarium;
- **container**—confined to a particular container, such as a pot or basket, grown either indoors or outdoors;
- **raised bed**—grown in a raised structure containing compost or piles of rotting wood;
- **community**—cultivated by a group of people, usually yielding fresh produce as well as a sense of community;
- **sensory**—designed to engage all the near and far senses; and
- **organic**—uses natural, sustainable gardening methods.[10]

Optimal growing conditions include the right combination of weather, environmental temperature, sunshine, soil moisture, and humidity. Microclimates, caused by "heat islands" or shady "cool spots," also impact the success or failure of gardens. Libraries that have no idea which plants would grow best in their region may want to consult the U.S. Department of Agriculture's (USDA) "plant hardiness zones," based on low temperature tolerance.[11] These zones help gardeners and farmers choose the plants that will most likely thrive in their area. For example, orchids need a tropical climate, while rhubarb grows best in temperate environments. The "hardiness zones" website provides detailed maps by ZIP code. National Resources Canada has its own hardiness zone maps, based on minimum temperature tolerance down to minus fifty-one degrees Celsius.[12]

Because the USDA can be slow to adapt to changing agricultural conditions, libraries may also want to consult the American Horticultural Society's (2018) "heat zone" map, based on more recent data about heat and drought conditions as well as new weather patterns. The zones reflect the number of days a year that a region experiences temperatures higher than eighty-six degrees—that is, the point at which plants begin suffering physiological damage from heat. Zone 1 is an area with less than one heat day a year, while Zone 12 has more than 210 heat days. Unfortunately, as informative as the USDA, National Resources Canada, and American Horticultural Society websites are, none of their maps account for microclimates, so libraries should always check with local nurseries, agricultural supply stores, the state agricultural extension program—and even neighbors!—to determine which plants to grow.

Plant Lists

Librarians may also want to confer with colleagues to see which plants they grow. Several libraries post their plant lists online as a service to visitors or as part of their demonstration garden efforts. The Master Gardeners of Benton and Franklin Counties (n.d.) has an extensive series of websites describing the plants in the Mid-Columbia Libraries' demonstration garden in Kennewick, Washington. Twenty-five different theme gardens, featuring more than 50 trees, 800 roses, and 100 shrubs, fill two acres behind the library. Each garden has its own website and is accompanied by an audio tour that describes the plants in that particular part of the overall demonstration garden. The websites and audio tours also detail the growing cycles of the various plants. Native bunchgrasses, for instance, grow actively in April, drop seeds in August, and dry up by September.[13]

Thanks in large part to the efforts of the local garden conservancy, the Landa branch library in San Antonio, Texas, is now a community center where children play and students read outdoors under shade trees. "The library and the grounds are a huge gathering place for families to come and meet other families," former conservancy president Ann Van Pelt noted. "The city needs a lot of places for children to run, play and, of course, to read books" (Mills 2012). The gardens surrounding the library have more than 7,000 plants, many of which are natives. Planting beds are grouped by seven themes: beauty and color, culinary herbs, medicinal, vegetables, perennials, fragrance, and grasses. The conservancy's online plant list makes a point of highlighting the garden's native plants.[14]

The plants in the NLM's medicinal herbal garden partially replicate Nicholas Culpeper's seminal work, *The Complete Herbal*, published in London in 1649. Of the almost 100 herbs featured in the NLM's garden, the following—and their healing properties—are described as part of an online plant list: chamomile, cinquefoil, columbine, feverfew, foxglove, golden rod, lady's mantle, lavender, lovage, pennyroyal, poppy, primrose, rosemary, sage, sorrel, vervain, wintergreen, woodruffe, and yarrow (U.S. National Library of Medicine 2016).

Water Matters

Even the hardiest drought-tolerant plants need water to survive. Therefore, providing the library's garden with an adequate yet environmentally responsible amount of water is a main concern. The Rosemary Garfoot Public Library (2007), the East Boston branch (Green Engineer 2017), and the Grand Rapids Public Library in Michigan all collect rainwater to hydrate their gardens (Jordan 2013, 103). In California, the Mill Valley Public Library harvests rainwater off the building's roof via a dry creek bed and rain tank. At Toronto's Centennial College, rainwater sustains an enormous living wall inside the library's atrium. The New River branch community garden, in Pasco County, Florida, prefers using rainwater because, as youth services provider Judy Curran insists, it's "healthier for plants than the treated water from the hose" (White 2016).

Other libraries use drip systems or timed sprinklers. Drip irrigation was installed in some parts of the Kennewick library's demonstration garden to avoid burning plant leaves with excess water. In other sections, tall sprinkler heads are high enough to prevent sprayed water from damaging flower blossoms.[15] A computerized drip system at the Tony Hillerman branch in Albuquerque alerts Rose Society members of any malfunctioning or broken hoses.[16] At San Francisco's Mission branch, a "smart drip" irrigation system reacts to weather conditions via satellite control (Eaton and Sullivan 2009).

LIBRARY RESOURCES

Gardening Tools

Libraries, especially those that have community gardens, often provide their gardeners with gardening equipment. The Northern Onondaga Public Library in Cicero, New York, makes tools and supplies available to gardeners who have plots at or work in the LibraryFarm's gardens. Shovels, rakes, a wheelbarrow, yard bags, and garbage bags are all stored in a shed that's accessible via a key kept at the circulation desk (LibraryFarm 2017). A cordless weed whacker and other gardening tools are also available to gardeners who work in the Westbank Libraries' community garden in Texas. Communal tools must be returned to their shed "dry and clean after use." Each gardener is assigned a separate shed bin for storing personal items (Westbank Community Garden 2018). In South Sioux City, Nebraska, the public library loans canning equipment so people working in the library's community gardens can preserve their bounty (Inklebarger 2016).

Some libraries even provide tools for community members to use in their own gardens. The Temescal branch of Oakland Public Library has one of the nation's oldest tool-lending libraries. Started in 2000, in response to community demand following both the Loma Prieta earthquake of 1989 and the Oakland Hills fire in 1991, the collection provides more than 5,000 tools to registered borrowers (Parr

2017). Available gardening tools include everything from an aerator to a bulb planter, from a fruit picker to a lawn edger, from lawn mowers to rakes, shovels, pruning shears, and something called a "mutt." Items can be checked out for up to seven days (Oakland Public Library n.d.). The Arlington Public Library, in Virginia, also lends gardening tools to library cardholders who are at least eighteen years old. Their tool collection, created to support the library's vegetable garden, includes a cuttlefish hoe, a dandelion weeder, an eleven-inch dibber, a fifty-inch Garden Weasel cultivator, and much more.[17] In its second year, the library loaned 340 gardening tools to some 200 borrowers (Vilelle 2017).

Book Collections

Tools, of course, aren't the only things libraries loan. In fact, gardening books have always been one of the most popular library collections. A library garden often goes hand in hand with having a strong gardening collection. The Albuquerque Rose Society regularly purchases gardening materials for the Tony Hillerman branch, where they also maintain multiple beloved rose gardens. The LSTA grant that funded El Dorado County Library's vegetable garden, in Northern California, also allowed staff to add more than 100 gardening books to its collection (Amos 2015). In Illinois, LSTA funded the purchase of print STEM materials, as well as the supplies needed to create two raised vegetable garden beds at the Stickney Forest View Public Library District (Austen 2016). And at the Arlington Heights Memorial Library, near Chicago, the young Sprout Squad not only cares for the library's small vegetable and herb garden, they also lend gardening and healthy eating books at the local farmers market.[18]

Some libraries even post seasonal lists of gardening books. "Now that warm weather is here to stay, it's time to get your garden ready," the Mid-Columbia Libraries' website announced. "Take a look at these books for ideas."[19] The Middle Country Public Library, in New York, provides an extensive book list in its *Growing Nature Literacy in Libraries Resource Book*, which is available online (Nature Explorium n.d.). Book listings, which include one-sentence annotations, are grouped by type (e.g., picture books, easy readers, nonfiction, and fiction) and grade level. Books for parents and educators are also listed.

CHALLENGES

Although no library program is completely problem-free, library gardens present their own unique brand of challenges. At the University of Western Illinois's Leslie F. Malpass Library, humidity caused by indoor foliage got so bad, at one point, that the library had to restrict the number of plants inside the building. Insects are also a problem since there are no natural predators inside the library.[20] Interior gardens provide other challenges as well. Plant containers occasionally leak, and the Washoe County Library, in Nevada, once had a rogue sprinkler. As a result, staff have learned not to shelve books under the hanging atrium planters.[21] Lush indoor greenery is also an excellent hiding place for drug paraphernalia and the like, plus staff at the Huntington Beach library have caught homeless men urinating in the indoor bushes. Small children have also fallen into the library's garden fountains.[22] Railings, which, according to one critic, ruin the architect's "effect," have since been installed at Huntington Beach (Bradley 2016).

As environmentally sound as rooftop gardens are, they can also be extremely problematic. The staff at the Salt Lake City Library recommend rethinking a rooftop garden to prevent the risk of leaks (Jordan 2013, 108). Indeed, in Highland, California, the leaky rooftop garden at the Sam J. Racadio Library and Environmental Learning Center had to be rebuilt after only eight years (Folmer 2018). *Celsus*, a self-proclaimed "library architecture source," cites Vancouver Public Library's original rooftop garden as a workable model. Fescue bunchgrass and kinnickinnick—chosen for their light weight when wet—were planted in fourteen inches of soil consisting of equal parts washed sand, pumice, and humus builder. The roof itself was covered in rubberized asphalt. Eight six-inch drains relieved the roof of any standing water ("Vancouver Public Library Rooftop Garden" 2010).

Conventional ground-level gardens present their own set of challenges too. Wildlife, such as birds and voles, eat the produce grown at the Pacifica-Sanchez branch in San Mateo County, California, while dogs and park visitors run through and trample the library's wildflower garden in Mill Valley.[23] At the Goldsboro branch of Wayne County Public Library, in North Carolina, staff and volunteers were devastated when someone toppled all the sunflowers growing in the library's garden (Edwards 2008). A different type of "vandalism" occurs at the Tony Hillerman branch, where community members assume it's okay to snip the library's beautiful roses. This is an especially chronic problem around Easter and Mother's Day, when staff have to gently intervene and remind would-be florists that the gardens are for everyone.[24]

In Brooklyn, the GreenBranches initiative actually helped reduce vandalism as young people became involved in garden workshops and activities. Allowing folks to visit the gardens after library hours remained an issue, however. "We want them to use [the garden]," children's librarian Valerie Garcia says. "But we're so short-staffed, we can't have anyone supervising it except during programming hours, so it's not safe" (Kuzyk 2007, 43).

NOTES

1. A. Doktor, personal communication, May 17, 2017.
2. Arlington Public Library, "Glencarlyn Branch Library Community Garden: A Teaching Garden," https://library.arlingtonva.us/explore/gardening-and-urban-famring/glencarlyn-garden.
3. S. Loney, personal communication, October 29, 2015.
4. S. Thompson, personal communication, August 1, 2018.
5. A. Brenner, personal communication, July 25, 2017.
6. S. Loney, personal communication, August 25, 2018.
7. J. Scott, personal communication, May 21, 2018.
8. LibraryFarm, Facebook page, www.facebook.com/LibraryFarm.
9. Centre for Excellence in Universal Design, "Universal Design," National Disability Authority, http://universaldesign.ie/What-is-Universal-Design/The-7-Principles/7-Principals-.pdf.
10. *Wikipedia*, "Gardening," https://en.wikipedia.org/wiki/Gardening.
11. Agricultural Research Service, "USDA Plant Hardiness Zone Map," https://planthardiness.ars.usda.gov.
12. Natural Resources Canada, "Plant Hardiness Zone Maps," www.planthardiness.gc.ca/?m=1&lang=en.
13. Washington State University Extension, "Native Plant Garden," posted December 20, 2013, https://extension.wsu.edu/benton-franklin/nativeplant.
14. Landa Gardens Conservancy, "Community Garden Plant List," https://landagardens.org/wp-content/uploads/2015/07/PlantList.pdf.
15. Washington State University Extension, "Border Garden," posted December 20, 2013, https://extension.wsu.edu/benton-franklin/border.
16. B. Farmer, personal communication, February 9, 2018.
17. Arlington Public Library, "Garden Tool Collection," https://libcat.arlingtonva.us/MyAccount/MyList/8739?_ga=2.252204553.1019764329.1533586242-431041959.1533586242.
18. T. Dantis, personal communication, June 27, 2017.
19. Mid-Columbia Libraries, "Gardening," www.midcolumbialibraries.org/gardening-0.
20. R. Fross, personal communication, May 16, 2018.
21. J. Andrews, personal communication, May 21, 2018.
22. S. Beverage, personal communication, July 26, 2018.
23. C. Vance, personal communication, July 6, 2017; A. Brenner, personal communication, July 25, 2017.
24. L. Metzer, personal communication, February 9, 2018.

CHAPTER SEVEN

Sustaining the Garden through Funding, Partnerships, and Volunteers

From grants to homegrown efforts, libraries use many different innovative ways to fund and sustain their gardens. While some are created in the memory of a beloved coworker or community member, others are the result of major fund-raising campaigns. Part of the Nature Explorium's start-up cost, for example, was raised through the Middle Country Public Library's Book Path initiative, where donors purchased bricks inscribed with a quote or the title of their favorite book (Lynch 2014, 25). Other libraries rely on the generosity of their Friends group or community partners. With a $500 grant from a local nonprofit organization, the Lansdowne Public Library, located in a suburb of Philadelphia, created a composting program where children fed leftover food waste to red wiggler worms. "We had all this compost," head of public services Abbe Klebanoff explains. "So I thought, 'Why don't we do a library garden?'" (27). She then acquired another $500 grant—this time from the Pennsylvania Horticultural Society—to plant tomatoes, peppers, and herbs in a small outdoor library garden.

However, as Raya Kuzyk (2007) points out, libraries "really can't sustain a garden unless enough people are dedicated to keeping it" (40). Indeed, in 2014, a team of horticultural researchers identified several challenges faced by the managers of demonstration gardens. Besides finding enough time to manage the garden, coordinators said they need more funding. Other hurdles include the lack of volunteers to work in the garden and not being able to enlist community partners. "Before beginning a garden project, consider and plan for the time and resources that will be required," they conclude. "Volunteer and community support is essential" (Glen et al. 2014). At one site in Northern California, funding and volunteer enthusiasm were robust the first two years of the library's gardening program but then slacked off substantially. The project manager is now responsible for finding funders to keep the garden going.[1] According to Mary Wilkins Jordan (2013), librarians not only need to find the resources to start a garden but also need to plan for sustainability. She goes on to urge staff to reach out into the community to identify partners and volunteers who can share ongoing expenses and help recruit gardeners.

FUNDING

Many, if not most, of the library gardens described in this book were initially funded through grants. Some of the grants were from large agencies, such as the IMLS and the ALSC, while the rest tended to be from local funders or community groups. The Berkeley County Library System (n.d.), in South Carolina, created its Sangaree Community Garden through a local grant funded by Home Depot plus support from the Sangaree special tax district. The Colonial Heights and Rancho Cordova branches of Sacramento Public Library created their food gardens thanks to a three-year grant from the Junior League of Sacramento.[2] The Chula Vista Public Library received a $20,000 "environmental and community engagement" grant from the Chula Vista Charitable Foundation to make the main library's parking lot more pedestrian friendly by restriping walkways and installing native plant gardens.[3] In Illinois, the Northlake Public Library created a "learning garden" with funds from a $5,000 Dollar General and ALSC grant. "We are grateful [to provide] 30 area children with an opportunity to learn to plant vegetables from seeds, construct a worm compost bin, dissect beans and seeds, learn about the web of life, and more," Marianne Ryczek, the library's head of youth services, exclaims ("Green Thumbs at Work" 2018).

Meanwhile, several libraries have benefited from government grants: Mill Valley and El Dorado County libraries, both in California, were awarded federal LSTA funds (Brenner 2015; Amos 2015), while Gwinnett County, in Georgia, got an IMLS Sparks! Ignition Grant for Libraries (IMLS 2018). Perhaps the most exciting project, however, is the Felton Library and Nature Discovery Park, anticipated to open in northern California in fall 2019. Called a "one-of-its-kind facility," the new branch will incorporate outdoor as well as indoor community spaces that promote environmental learning. Funding for the project comes from a $395,000 California State Department of Parks and Recreation grant, county-wide library bond measure monies, and a $1 million grant from the state's general fund (Dwire 2018; Ibarra 2018). "The role of libraries is changing to offer communities a broader range of innovative services," Santa Cruz County Library director Susan Nemitz says. "The Felton Library and Nature Discovery Park accomplishes this" ("Calif. Contributes $1M" 2018).

Libraries also depend on the kindness of Friends as well as local businesses and community agencies. At the Goldsboro branch of the Wayne County Public Library, in North Carolina, a garden was started via contributions from the Friends of the Library and the parks and recreation department. These gifts were then parlayed into a $3000 summer reading grant from ALSC, which helped the library create a productive food garden (Edwards 2008). Likewise, in the small town of Pacifica, California, several businesses provided funds and materials to start a food garden at the local branch of the San Mateo County Libraries. Wells Fargo bank pitched in $1000, while an Ace Hardware store donated lumber to build the raised garden beds. A plant nursery gave soil and a tree service company provided mulch.[4] In Queens, New York, the Women's Club of Malba donated $25,000 to maintain the reading garden at the Whitestone library. According to first vice president Rosemarie Scarola, the club decided to support the library's garden by providing funds that "will directly impact the community in a meaningful way" (Suriel 2015).

Some projects garner money from targeted fund-raising campaigns. An impressive list of donors helped defray half the initial $300,000 cost of the Nature Explorium. Major funders supported specific aspects of the project: for instance, the Bank of America helped pay for the children's "Create It" area, while the Allstate Foundation contributed toward the "Willow Tunnel." Other donations came from the library's Friends, the chamber of commerce, four foundations, three banks, and two grants from local legislators.[5] So, too, was Glendale's xeriscape demonstration garden funded by various partner organizations. Art installations enliven the garden thanks to the Glendale Water Conservation Office, which received an "Art in the Garden" grant from the National Endowment for the Arts, Arizona Commission on the Arts, and the city of Glendale. Interpretive signage was provided by the Arizona Game and Fish Department's Heritage Fund, plus the garden features a 3,000-square-foot Desert Food Forest courtesy of an Arizona Department of Forestry and Fire Management grant.[6] In Saint Paul, Minnesota, the Sun Ray Library and Conway Park demonstration project was funded by the National Fish and Wildlife Foundation as well as through a Wells Fargo "Environmental Solutions for Communities" grant (C&NN 2015).

Leslie F. Malpass Library, Western Illinois University
Photo credit: Photography by Julia A. Thompson, Malpass Library employee

Other fund-raising efforts may include special events or ongoing campaigns. Since 1991, the Friends of the Mt. Lebanon Public Library, in Pennsylvania, have sponsored an annual garden tour to benefit the library, including its gardens. Over the years, more than $538,000 has been raised.[7] And at the Western Illinois University, the Library Atrium Society—named after the Leslie F. Malpass Library's amazing indoor garden—solicits memberships to support collections and services. The society promises to name an atrium plant in honor of anyone who contributes $1,000 or more to the fund.[8]

Library gardens may also benefit from bequests or memorials. The Zion-Benton Public Library, north of Chicago, established its garden to memorialize a former library trustee, while in New York money was donated specifically to create a garden in memory of the Rochester Public Library board president's daughter (Jordan 2013, 104). Nearby, on Long Island, the Sachem Public Library's Inside/Out garden was made possible thanks to a monetary legacy left by Mary M. Martinez, a longtime employee of the library. She wanted others to "enjoy the rewards in knowledge, enrichment, and happiness" offered by the library and so her bequest was used to transform the library's parking lot into a public garden (Vaccaro 2010). The Waterford Township Public Library, in Michigan, used $5,000 in memorial funds to create a sensory garden in front of the library (Hopkins 2015). More recently, a garden and reading bench were dedicated in memory of Mary Bourguignon, at the Fairfield Civic Center branch of the Solano County Library in California. Bourguignon was campaign manager for a library measure that successfully passed in 1998 and was executive director of the library's foundation. "It is exciting to create a new community space," library director Bonnie Katz shared. "It is a wonderful way to honor Mary and extend to the outdoors the library's mission of sparking curiosity, inspiring creativity, and championing learning. I think Mary would be proud" (Hiland 2018).

PARTNERSHIPS

"It's easy to get a grant to start stuff," an academic partner advises, "but you need someone to keep it going" (Lynch 2014). A garden planted at Tucson's Davis Bilingual Elementary School, in 1994, fell into disrepair until faculty and the community took a renewed interest in the project. Today the school hosts eleven plots, including native desert and pollinator plants, in addition to an aquaponics garden in the library.[9] Likewise, in Arlington, Virginia, local Master Gardeners took over a Boy Scout gardening project several years after it was abandoned. The rejuvenated Glencarlyn Library Community Garden is now rife with flora and is used by the library as a teaching space (Mills 2018; Master Gardeners of Northern Virginia n.d.).

Like the Three Sisters of Haudenosaunee (Iroquois) stories, library gardens flourish when partners work together to accomplish a common goal. As the story goes, three sisters, representing corn, beans, and squash, sprang from the grave of Sky

Woman's daughter. They bickered and were sometimes separated, but in the end, the sisters came together to support one another and nourish the People (Broderick and Jordan 2017). The Three Sisters story and the Brown County Library's Cellcom Children's Edible Garden, in Wisconsin, both exemplify the role of garden partners. In this case, the purpose of Brown County's garden is to provide "a hands-on learning environment that supports and reinforces literacy and learning."[10] Funds for the library garden were initially donated by a corporate sponsor (i.e., wireless provider Cellcom), with additional money raised through grants. Subsequent partners, who help maintain the garden, include

- Boy Scouts, who built three planters;
- local Master Gardeners, who work in the garden;
- the Rotary Club, which holds seed drives;
- Syble Hopp School students, who germinate the seeds in their greenhouse;
- various local businesses that donated craft supplies, signage, and hardscape;
- St. Norbert College "Into the Streets" volunteers; and
- Brown County 4-H and University of Wisconsin Extension volunteers (Brown County Library 2015; Liebergen n.d.)

A separate group of partners presents gardening programs at the library. These partners include the Greenbay Botanical Garden, the Brown County Parks Department, and members of the Oneida Nation, who share the story of the Three Sisters.

This wide range of partnerships is typical of library gardens and allows libraries to extend their services beyond their own capabilities. Libraries bring to the table "solid community connections, stature as highly trusted institutions, capacity to deliver programs and distribute information to large and diverse audiences," as well as universal accessibility (Urban Libraries Council 2013, 111). Library partners bring their own expertise, connections, money, volunteers, and goodwill. Like the relationship among the Three Sisters, each partner benefits.

Potential garden partners abound at the national and local levels. For example, the goal of Nature Explore is to transform "children's lives through research-based classroom design, services, educator workshops, and natural products."[11] The organization has provided this expertise to several libraries, including the Nature Explorium, the Anythink libraries in Colorado, and the Nature Explore Center at the Finney County Public Library in Kansas. As a result, children are able to experience nature in all these spaces, even in commercial and suburban areas. At one Anythink library, a child who was participating in a gardening program exclaimed, "This plant smells like squash!," confirming her ability to make subtle observations (Lane 2015). An initiative similar to Nature Explore is the Children & Nature Network, whose vision is to create a "world in which all children play, learn and grow with nature in their everyday lives."[12] In addition to various funding partners, C&NN collaborated with the Saint Paul Public Library to help create a "Natural Library" at the Sun Ray branch.

The C&NN-guided project provides environmental education through programs and collections and by developing young leaders. Library activities in the adjacent park, a nature-themed winter book club, and a pollinator garden are all results of C&NN's influence (Otto 2016).

Museums, Botanical Gardens, and Parks

As useful as national organizations can be, the vast majority of partnerships begin at the local level. An outstanding example is the astonishing forest garden of the François Mitterand Library (FML), which partners with the French National Museum of Natural History. The FML surrounds a two-and-a-half-acre forest that is open on top but closed to the public to protect the plants and "insure the peace of the readers." The Natural History Museum worked with FML to design the forest and continues to help with maintenance. Museum personnel also monitor the numerous flora and fauna that live in the forest: as of 2009, fifty-eight types of plants, twenty-eight different sorts of insects, and twelve bird species. The forest plays many roles at the library, including providing a place of quiet contemplation, and is ever "mysterious and magical, unreachable but always there" (Bibliothèque nationale de France n.d.).[13]

Botanical gardens are also a good source of expertise, volunteers, and even plants. When Brooklyn Public Library decided to create its first garden in 1999, Carrie, as head of the library's former "The Child's Place for Children with Special Needs" (now Inclusive Services) department, reached out to the Brooklyn Botanic Garden (BBG) for help with testing the soil, marking the start of a years-long partnership that continues to benefit both agencies to this day. Through its community outreach program, BBG provided compost bins, free and discounted plants, and, in 2001, a completely renovated garden that served as a model for accessible gardening in a small space. In partnership with BBG, the library became a founding member of a horticultural therapy round table that brought together people from Brooklyn's special education programs, hospitals, veterans services, senior centers and nursing homes, and the Rikers Island Correctional Facility to discuss common concerns. Carrie also provided inclusion training to BBG staff and volunteers. She and BBG even teamed up to make a joint presentation on creating barrier-free gardens and inclusive garden programming at a national Gardening Association conference.

Other U.S. public libraries, including Chicago and Mt. Lebanon, have worked with their local botanical gardens; but only one library is actually located inside a botanical garden: the Library in a Garden, member of the Jefferson County Public Library Cooperative in Birmingham, Alabama. Founded as part of the garden in 1973, the library became a member of the cooperative in 1978, gaining databases and cataloging services, the ability to partner with other libraries for grants, and a

Fairy garden at the Library in the Garden at the Birmingham Botanical Garden, Alabama

Photo credit: Friends of Birmingham Botanical Garden

broader audience. In exchange, the cooperative gets access to a deeper and more specialized collection on gardening, nature, and the natural history of Alabama, the fifth most biodiverse state in the United States. "The Library in the Garden is all about books, bugs, birds, bees, plants, and trees," says director Hope Long, and offers resources that students can borrow and take with them on "field trips" to the botanical garden itself. One highlight is the George Washington Carver collection, which encourages youngsters, grades one through six, to explore his life via the library's archives before going out into the garden to harvest peanuts, sweet potatoes, and cotton. The library also offers a seed exchange and "Thyme to Read" book club for adults.[14]

Much larger, but similarly situated, is Mexico's national library, la Biblioteca Vasconcelos, which is surrounded by a botanical garden containing 60,000 plants, including many on the roof. Designed in partnership with the National Autonomous University of Mexico, the library was built amid a barren landscape in the middle of Mexico City. The surrounding gardens are "part of an attempt at urban ecological regeneration" (Meinhold 2010). According to one reviewer, "The botanical garden, just like the books and computers inside the library is a source of knowledge and acts to educate the visitors of the library" (Meinhold 2010).

Parks, too, can be valuable partners. Libraries in Arlington Heights, Illinois, and Saint Paul, Minnesota (Otto 2016), and the proposed new library in Felton, California (Ibarra 2018), all benefit from cooperative relationships with nearby parks.[15] Karen McIntyre, school library media specialist at the Westmeade Elementary School in Tennessee, expanded the library's garden by creating the Young Naturalist Program in conjunction with the nearby Warner Park Nature Center. Three times a year, each grade visits the Nature Center, where park staff conduct hands-on activities. Together, McIntyre and the center staff developed a curriculum, trained faculty, identified the plants and animals on the school campus, and helped prepare the case for certifying the library's garden as a wildlife habitat.[16]

Internal Partnerships

An important, but often overlooked source of partnerships is coworkers and fellow departments in one's own institution. The Sam W. Hitt Medicinal Plant Gardens, at the University of North Carolina, works with the campus biology department (GAEA Project n.d.). Likewise, the Greenfield Community College's Nahman-Watson Library partners with the science department and campus greenhouse to offer a seed library (Solomon 2017). In San Diego County, the Pauma Band of Luiseño Indians library shares a building with an afterschool program. Together they started a garden in hopes of getting kids to go outside. The library funded and supervised the garden, while the afterschool program participants tended the plants. The garden, which started as a twenty-square-foot plot, eventually grew to a quarter acre with a homemade greenhouse and drip irrigation system. Enough vegetables were grown that all produce was offered to the community for free.[17]

Meanwhile, back at the Westmeade Elementary School, media specialist Karen McIntyre relates how, while trying to engage faculty, she was approached by the physical education teacher about creating a joint program that would promote exercise and healthy eating. Together they successfully submitted a small grant request that allowed them to build two raised beds. From there, McIntyre was able to use the garden to tie in with the teachers' curricula. In one instance, a connection to a social studies assignment was made through early ink. "The Constitution was written in pokeberry ink," she explains. "We made the ink and then wrote with it." For McIntyre, there is a deep synergy between the library and the garden. "Both inspire curiosity, questioning and learning," she says. "When kids are outside and experiencing, it is a jumping off point for questions and answers." Today, the garden is connected to every department on campus, which is well on its way to becoming a Sustainability Magnet School, the first for Tennessee.[18]

VOLUNTEERS

Sources of Volunteers

One of the functions of a good partnership is helping to recruit volunteer gardeners. A vital source of volunteers is Master Gardener programs, which are active in most states and, through international affiliation, in most Canadian provinces. Master Gardeners are certified by agricultural extension programs that are, themselves, the result of partnerships between the U.S. Department of Agriculture and land grant universities. Library gardens from California to New York rely on the guidance and work ethic of Master Gardeners. The Montgomery County Master Gardeners, in Maryland, recruit volunteers for the National Museum of Health and Medicine's garden. Nearby Master Gardeners also created and oversee a teaching garden at the public library in Boonsboro. The Master Gardeners at Forsyth County Public Library, in Georgia, run the gardens at three branches, doing everything from fund-raising, planning, weeding, programming, and even hosting picnics for the occasional researcher. In Washington, Master Gardeners are responsible for maintaining the Mid-Columbia Libraries' stellar demonstration garden in Kennewick. A list of Master Gardener programs and their international affiliates is available online.[19]

Aquaponic garden at Davis Bilingual Elementary School
Photo credit: Moses Thompson

Besides their connections to Master Gardener programs, universities and colleges may also provide interns or students who need to complete community service hours before graduating. The gardens at the Davis Bilingual Elementary School have an excellent partnership with the University of Arizona, which sends six "school and community gardening" interns to the school every semester. "One of our goals is to relate things in the garden to things they're learning in school," one project intern says. "Math lessons about spacing and sizing of the plants. Science lessons about learning to observe plants and predict what might happen to them" (D'Andre 2014).

Another source for recruiting garden volunteers is the Corporation for National and Community Service (CNCS), which was created by Congress and runs programs such as RSVP (Retired Senior Volunteer Program) and AmeriCorps.[20] Boy Scouts and Girl Scouts can also be helpful resources. ScoutingUSA has sponsored five garden projects at the Mt. Lebanon Public Library, and Girl Scout Troop 1225 has been instrumental in making Westmeade Elementary School's garden a success. Local scout chapters can be found through their websites.[21]

Groups, such as fraternities, sororities, the Junior League, and faith-based organizations have all provided library garden volunteers. Some of the volunteers that help maintain the garden at the César E. Chávez branch, in Oakland, come from a social services agency that assists individuals with developmental disabilities.[22] The Carnegie Library of Pittsburgh frequently lists gardening opportunities on its volunteer recruitment webpage.[23] The listing is cross-posted on the Pittsburgh Cares website, which is a clearinghouse for volunteer opportunities throughout the city.[24] At the Brooklyn Public Library, young Book Buddies are encouraged, through Volunteer Services and local branches, to also consider working in the library's gardens. School library media centers might want to model themselves after the Westmeade and Maria Garza elementary schools and initiate afterschool gardening clubs.

Volunteer Job Descriptions and Retention

While some tasks, like deadheading roses or watering, are clearly defined, others, such as managing the garden, are less so. The volunteer's role, levels of independence, and the need for supervision may vary greatly from one garden to the next. Anthony was a teen with autism who volunteered at the Inclusive Services garden at the Sunset Park branch in Brooklyn. Although, as Carrie observed, he was not a gardener, he was a fluid interpreter of English into both Cantonese and Mandarin and so, with supervision, provided a valuable bridge to the Chinese-speaking communities in that neighborhood.

Well-written volunteer job descriptions reduce the frustration of recruitment by telling people exactly what to expect. The garden volunteer job description of Plaistow Public Library, in New Hampshire, is short but effective, briefly listing all the essential information needed by potential library gardeners:

> ## GARDENERS
>
> *Session runs from May to October.*
>
> We need volunteers to help care for our lawn and develop gardens. Volunteers will regularly water, weed, dig, mulch and prune, according to the needs of the garden.
>
> — **Who** —
> Our volunteers work on their own and like to bend, lift and dig in the dirt. Prior home gardening experience is an asset.
>
> — **When** —
> Flexible schedule. All shifts must occur when Library is open.[25]

The Sycamore Library, in Illinois, takes a more reward-based approach, but its job description is equally effective:

> Our More Than Books Community Garden is a space where members of the community are able to learn, discover, create, and grow together. As a garden volunteer you can meet new people, share your skills, and get a little dirty in the process. Whether you are an experienced green thumb or are new to the gardening scene, this is an opportunity for you to give back to your community in a meaningful way. Those who volunteer are able to take home the fruits of their labor. Whatever remains goes to the local food pantry to help those in need.[26]

Sycamore's volunteer application asks very specific questions about gardening experience, skills (e.g., planting, construction, harvesting, weeding, none), knowledge of gardening practices (e.g., none, basic, strong), physical ability to carry out gardening tasks, and availability.[27] (For the complete application form, see appendix C).

Once the match between volunteer and assignment is made, the garden work should be as rewarding for the volunteer as it is useful for the library. Volunteer services expert Carla Lehn (2016) reminds us, "Your best shot at retention is to be sure you meet the volunteer's needs, not just yours" (36). Making the job rewarding starts with understanding the volunteers' motivation. Are they looking for employment experience or academic credit? Are they hoping to fulfill a volunteer or service learning requirement? Or do they just love to garden? The desire to create change can be especially motivating for baby boomers, who welcome the "opportunity to empower others and address the social needs in their community" (Powe 2016, 151). Whatever the motivation is, make sure the library can provide what's needed to keep all volunteers engaged.

The right match between gardener, garden, and motivation can be magical. Judy, a longtime volunteer who had schizophrenia, worked at the Flatlands branch in Brooklyn for ten years. She kept the garden alive during drought and staff shortages. As she explains,

> I love being a volunteer at the library because I have a chance to change my lifestyle and contribute to other people when I'm needed. Usually, my life centers around therapy all week long. However, for two hours each week I have the opportunity to apply myself to my work skills and also socialize with the nicest people. . . . I like gardening and I hope I am doing a satisfactory job. I like thinking that I am delighting children if the garden is flourishing. (Banks 2016, 209)

NOTES

1. J. Stockinger, personal communication, May 17, 2017.
2. Ibid.
3. S. Loney, personal communication, August 25, 2017.
4. C. Vance, personal communication, July 6, 2017.
5. For a list of Nature Explorium donors, see Middle Country Library Foundation, "Sponsors, Supporters, Donors," www.middlecountrylibraryfoundation.com/pdf/SponsorbenefitForm.pdf.
6. City of Glendale, Arizona, "Water Conservation—Xeriscape Demonstration Garden," www.glendaleaz.com/waterconservation/xeriscapegarden.cfm.
7. Mt. Lebanon Public Library, "Garden Tour," https://mtlebanonlibrary.org/463/Garden-Tour.
8. Western Illinois University, "Library Atrium Society," www.wiu.edu/libraries/administration/development/atriumsociety.php.
9. A. Edgette, personal communication, November 17, 2017.
10. Brown County Library, "Cellcom Children's Edible Garden @ Central Library," www.browncountylibrary.org/kids/garden.
11. Nature Explore, https://natureexplore.org.
12. Children & Nature Network, "Vision and Mission," www.childrenandnature.org/about.
13. The text of the quotes in this paragraph has been translated and paraphrased by the authors from the original French (Bibliothèque nationale de France n.d.).
14. Birmingham Botanical Gardens "The Library at The Gardens," www.bbgardens.org/library.php.
15. T. Danton, personal communication, June 27, 2017.
16. Young Naturalists @ Westmeade, "Help Make Westmeade Tennessee's 1st Sustainability Magnet," www.westmeade.net/our-natural-history-museum.html.
17. J. Zagarella, personal communication, August 16, 2018.

18. K. McIntyre, personal communication, February 14, 2018.
19. eXtension, "State and Provincial Master Gardener Programs: Extension and Affiliated Program Listings," https://articles.extension.org/pages/9925/state-and-provincial-master-gardener-programs:-extension-and-affiliated-program-listings.
20. Corporation for National and Community Service, www.nationalservice.gov.
21. Boy Scouts of America, "Find Scouting Near You," https://beascout.scouting.org and Girl Scouts, https://joingirlscouts.org.
22. P. Villaseñor, personal communication, June 15, 2018.
23. Carnegie Library of Pittsburgh, "Volunteer," www.carnegielibrary.org/donate/volunteer-at-the-library.
24. Pittsburgh Cares, www.pittsburghcares.org.
25. Plaistow Public Library, "Volunteer Positions: Gardeners," www.plaistowlibrary.com/volunteer.asp#gardenervolunteer.
26. Sycamore Library, "Get Involved," www.sycamorelibrary.org/get-involved.
27. Sycamore Library, "Garden Volunteer Application," www.sycamorelibrary.org/garden-volunteer-application.

CHAPTER EIGHT

Evaluating Garden Programs

All library programs are worthwhile or libraries wouldn't offer them. But sometimes library staff need to prove the value of programs to administrators, governing bodies, and funders. When Wayne County Public Library children's librarian Shorlette Ammons-Stephens approached her library director about starting a community garden, the director responded, "What does that have to do with the library?" Nevertheless, Ammons-Stephens prevailed and was able to acquire funding from the library's Friends as well as from the local parks and recreation department. She also began collecting evidence showing how the garden helped foster a sense of community. Residents soon noticed that the library was growing food and so began asking if they could take some home. One community member, with recipe in hand, even showed staff what she had cooked using the library's produce. Citing this anecdote, Ammons-Stephens submitted a successful summer reading program grant application to the ALSC and received $3,000 to continue the garden. "The money is great, but they're acknowledging how special the program is," library director Jane Rustin proclaims. "That is what was so sweet to me" (Edwards 2008).

The advantages of measuring, or evaluating, the effectiveness of library services are many. A well-constructed evaluation tells the library

- whether it has met its program goals,
- what changes need to occur to improve the library's services, and
- what impact the library's programs and services have on the community.

As demonstrated in Wayne County, evaluation results can also be used to justify the existence and maybe even the expansion of certain programs, like community gardens. And yet, when Master Gardeners in North Carolina were asked how they evaluate their services, 35 percent of respondents said they don't evaluate them (Glen et al. 2014). This percentage would likely be even higher if librarians were asked how they evaluate their garden programs.

REPORTING NUMBERS

Library staff are expert at reporting numbers related to workload. They know intimately how many items are checked out from their collection, how many people attend their programs, how many reference questions they answer, and how many people visit the library. These measurements are called "outputs" and are usually compiled as annual statistics. Outputs are important because they record the volume of work that library staff accomplish. Equally important are "inputs," which are the amount of internal resources the library uses to provide services. These include the number of staff employed, the size of the collection, the number of available computers and meeting rooms, the number of programs offered, and the number of library volunteers. These figures are often compared to other libraries' inputs to validate an institution's deficits and strengths.

An outstanding example of garden-related inputs and outputs is the annual report of the Friends of the Birmingham Botanical Gardens (2015), which also supports The Library at The Gardens. Among the statistics reported are the number of children and adult programs conducted and how many people attend (almost 25,000 participated in nearly 1,000 programs over fiscal year 2014–2015), the amount of contact hours (i.e., the number of "hours of interaction" between program participants and instructors), the percentage of programs offered for free, and the number of volunteers and total hours they donate (over 1,000 volunteers donated more than 30,000 hours in fiscal year 2014–2015). In addition, the report provides detailed attendance tallies for every program conducted and whether these figures are higher or lower than those from the previous year. Some of the programs offered include "Hikes for Tykes," "Earth Day at the Gardens," "Thyme to Read Book Club," "Gross-Out Camp," and "Garden Explorations" (Friends of Birmingham Botanical Gardens 2015). The Friends use these data to help plan the following year's program agenda.

PROGRAM OUTCOMES

As vital as inputs and outputs are for planning the future, as well as for reporting past performance, they still don't capture the *value* of an institution's services. For this reason, many funders, including IMLS, now require grantees to report the outcomes of grant projects. Unlike inputs and outputs, which are strictly quantitative, outcomes describe the positive change that happens as a result of using the library. Change may occur from gaining a new or enhanced skill, acquiring new knowledge, taking on a different or improved attitude, modifying a behavior, or improving a condition or life status. Possible outcomes that might occur as a result of participating in garden programs include learning how to compost (new skill); understanding the role milkweed plays in a butterfly's life cycle (new knowledge); suddenly appreciating how climate change impacts planting seasons (change in attitude); eating healthier food after tasting library-grown vegetables (change in behavior); and becoming a Master Gardener after volunteering a requisite number of hours in the library's garden (change in status). Carrie provides two real-life examples of library garden outcomes: As a result of attending an inclusive program at a Brooklyn Public Library garden, parents reported that their children interacted more appropriately with other children than they do when at nongarden programs (i.e., improved behavior). Likewise, a teen volunteer with an intellectual disability became a role model for young attendees by regularly leading art activities at inclusive garden sessions (i.e., change in status).

Outcomes describe the benefits the library provides its users. Therefore, identifying the desired outcome before planning a program is critical if a library wants to make a positive impact on the community. In their book on outcome-based planning and evaluation (OBPE), Melissa Gross, Cindy Mediavilla, and Virginia A. Walter (2016) outline the following five steps to providing effective library services:

1. **Gathering information** about the community, as well as the library's capacity to take on something new
2. **Determining outcomes** based on the information gathered
3. **Developing programs and services** to achieve the targeted outcomes
4. **Conducting evaluations** to measure accomplishment of the outcomes
5. **Leveraging the library's role** in the community—and with administrators and funders—based on what was achieved or still needs to be achieved (6)

These five steps can easily be applied to planning and evaluating library garden programs.

OUTCOME-BASED PLANNING

Identifying community priorities and aspirations (i.e., OBPE step 1) should always be the first step in planning any new library service. Some of this information might be gleaned through observation or research. But often the best way to learn what residents want is to ask them. Many of the libraries in this book initiated community gardens because their users live in food deserts—that is, neighborhoods that lack access to fresh fruit, vegetables, and other healthful foods, due largely to a dearth of grocery stores or other healthy food providers (American Nutrition Association 2010). As people who work in the community, library staff may be keenly aware of the lack of supermarkets and green spaces in the surrounding neighborhood. The full meaning of these observations may not occur to them, however, until they hear parents say that their children have no idea where food comes from. At that point, library staff might start wondering how the library can help bring healthier food to the community.

Once community members' priorities are identified, the library can then target particular outcomes, or goals, to help residents achieve their aspirations (OBPE step 2). Let's say, for instance, that in talking with parents, the children's librarian discovers that there is a shared concern over childhood obesity. The children's librarian does some research and finds a recent study confirming that many families need to be taught how and why to eat healthier food (Florida 2018). Thus, the library might set as its goal "Families learn to eat healthy food." The statement not only presents a positive outcome (i.e., learning to eat healthy food) but also specifies who will benefit (i.e., families). This is a viable outcome because it promises a positive gain in *knowledge*, one of the six types of change that define outcomes.

In targeting the outcome, staff also need to consider the library's capacity for achieving the proposed change. How exactly can the library help families learn about eating healthy foods? There are many ways to achieve this outcome, including offering classes on nutrition, providing field trips to farmers markets, and giving families the opportunity to experience fresh-grown vegetables. For the purposes of this hypothetical case study, staff decide to create a community garden where families can grow food and attend healthy-living programs. Indeed, as Mary Wilkins Jordan (2013) suggests, gardens serve their communities by providing

- a source of fresh fruits, vegetables, and herbs that address food security;
- a source of physical activity that promotes health and relaxation; and
- an important link to nature in an urban setting. (102)

At the El Dorado County Library, in California, staff tackled the obesity issue by offering the "Growing Teens: Community Garden" project, funded through an LSTA grant. First, the targeted group of teens learned about gardening and how to build raised vegetable beds. Next, they actually constructed garden beds and planted seeds, which they were then responsible for cultivating. When the vegetables were ready to be picked, the rookie gardeners harvested, cooked, and ate what they had grown. Every activity associated with the project was designed to achieve the ultimate goal of teaching young people how to grow and eat healthy food (OBPE step 3). In fact, several outcomes were achieved by the end of the program: the teens reported eating more nutritious meals (i.e., change in behavior); they described a higher level of awareness in their overall eating habits (i.e., increased knowledge); plus they gained healthy cooking skills (new skills) (Amos 2015).

Other library garden programs resulting in similar outcomes include Gwinnett County Public Library's "Homegrown Gwinnett" program, which uses aquaponic towers to grow vegetables at every branch (IMLS 2018); the Portland High School library's garden, in Tennessee, that provides healthy food for the pantry that serves a third of the school's students and their families[1]; and the STEM Garden that grew pizza toppings and herbs at the Stickney Forest View Public Library District in Illinois (Austen 2016). All of these projects were motivated by a need to teach community members how to eat healthier food.

MEASURING RESULTS

Each garden in this book serves a distinct purpose, whether it's to demonstrate native plants or supply produce to community food pantries, make the library building more energy efficient, or just provide a peaceful place to sit and contemplate nature. These are all worthy goals, but how do libraries know they have achieved them (OBPE step 4)? In El Dorado County, staff conducted pre- and post-test surveys as well as interviews to evaluate whether or not their project outcomes had been met. Gwinnett County, on the other hand, relied heavily on output measures and anecdotal evidence to demonstrate the success of its aquaponic gardens. In only six months, nearly 2,200 Gwinnett County residents, of all ages and ethnicities, attended some 120 programs related to gardening and healthy living. Community participation in and enthusiasm for the project far exceeded initial expectations. "The programming has really knocked our socks off," project coordinator Meg Wilson explains. After attending the library's various garden-related programs, many participants were overheard saying, "I didn't know libraries do things like this" (IMLS 2018).

Evaluations can be conducted in several different ways. The most common techniques are these:

- Analyzing outputs
- Administering surveys
- Conducting interviews
- Conducting focus groups
- Recording observations

As illustrated in figure 8.1, most of these methods are helpful in evaluating achievement of one or more types of outcomes.

Output Analysis

Funders and administrators will want to know how many people visit the library's garden and participate in gardening programs. Therefore, it is important that libraries collect these data, even if they do not directly reflect outcomes. Staff know how to tally library program attendance; but collecting the number of people who visit a garden can be tricky, especially if the space is not monitored. We recommend scheduling week-long sample periods to record a representative number of people visiting the garden throughout the year. Counts should be collected at various times of the week to form as complete a visitation picture as possible. For example, you might want to tally visitors at 1:00 p.m. on Monday, 3:30 p.m. on Wednesday, 10:30 a.m. on Thursday, 11:00 a.m. on Saturday, and, if the library is open, at 2:00 p.m. on Sunday. By counting visitors at various times, certain usage patterns may arise. When, for example, is the garden busiest: At lunchtime on weekdays? Right after school? Or is it most crowded on the weekend? If possible, one sample week should be scheduled per season to capture year-round usage. The tallies can then be multiplied by the remaining number of weeks in the season to estimate how many people visit the garden and when.

FIGURE 8.1
Evaluation techniques to measure outcomes

EVALUATION TECHNIQUES	OUTCOMES	EXAMPLES
Outputs	N/A	• Count the number of adults/children who attend a gardening program. • Count the number of people who visit the garden.
Surveys	Attitude Behavior Knowledge Status/condition	• Ask respondents' level of confidence in being able to plant vegetables. (attitude) • Ask teens how their eating habits have changed as a result of attending library programs on nutrition. (behavior) • Ask children to name or draw pictures of three pollinators. (knowledge) • Ask adult volunteers how their health has improved as a result of working in the library's garden. (condition).
Interviews	Attitude Behavior Knowledge Status/condition	• Ask teenagers how they feel about climate change. (attitude) • Ask children which vegetables they now eat after tasting produce from the library's garden. (behavior) • Ask adults to name local native plants. (knowledge) • Ask adults how at peace they feel after visiting the library's contemplative garden. (condition)
Focus groups	Attitude Behavior Knowledge Status/condition	• Ask a group of adults to describe the advantages of eating organic foods. (attitude/knowledge) • Ask a group of parents to describe how their children's eating habits have changed as a result of participating in the library's healthy-living program. (behavior) • Ask a class of fourth-graders how their math grades have improved as a result of participating in the library's STEM garden programs. (status)
Observation	Behavior Skill	• Watch children play in the garden. Are they more engaged outside the library than they are inside? (behavior) • Watch teens working in the garden. Are they more adept at planting seeds at the end of the planting season than they were at the beginning? (skill)

Although outputs do not measure value or impact, they can be useful in tracking usage and participation. They also provide baseline data when comparing usage patterns from year to year, season to season, and even day to day. Lower attendance rates, for instance, may prompt staff to use other evaluation methods to figure out why attendance is declining. Outputs also give quantitative context to the program's overall results. For example, El Dorado County targeted twenty-five teens to participate in its community garden program: Did they all participate in every aspect of the program, or did some dropout and, if so, why?

Surveys

Perhaps the most common way to assess the impact of library programs is through surveys. Questionnaires are anonymous and generally nonthreatening, plus they are relatively easy to administer. Surveys are also a good way to track immediate changes in knowledge and attitude as well as longer-term changes in behavior, skill, condition, and life status. Assessing what was learned during a program on nutrition, for instance, can be accomplished by administering the same survey twice, right before the presentation and then again directly afterward. Immediate knowledge gains are measured by comparing the two sets of responses: Were attendees able to list a greater number of nutritious foods on the post-test survey than they could before the program? A different survey instrument might then be sent to the same attendees several weeks later to see if their eating habits had changed as a result of attending the program. Responses to the follow-up survey would then be used to measure a change in behavior.

The Public Library Association has created a generic follow-up instrument as part of its Project Outcome initiative. Survey questions include "I used what I learned to complete a task or goal" and "I used what I learned to do something new or different." Respondents answer the questions with either "yes," "no" or "not applicable" and are asked to explain their responses. The follow-up surveys can be administered either by e-mail or text, via a phone interview, or in person. Whether you use PLA's instruments or your own, following up with participants requires that you collect contact information (either e-mail addresses or text/phone numbers) during the initial event being evaluated. PLA provides a clear description of this process in its "Project Outcome: Follow-Up Survey Protocol" (Project Outcome 2017).

Interviews

As easy as it is to administer surveys, responding to a written questionnaire can be far more difficult than one may think. Surveys are impersonal, noninteractive, and require respondents to be able to read the questions, which are usually written in English. For these reasons, some libraries prefer seeking participant feedback via interviews, either face-to-face or by telephone. Like survey questions, interview questions are developed in advance but can be expanded upon or modified if clarification is needed. Interviews also tend to be conversational and so lend themselves to more informal encounters. Instead of distributing intrusive—not to mention impractical!—paper surveys to people visiting the garden, staff might want to engage visitors in a friendly conversation about their garden experience: What benefits do they get from visiting the garden?

Interviews are also a good way to get feedback from children, who might not yet read or be able to understand a written survey. Youngsters respond better to fun encounters, so evaluators will want to provide an activity, like drawing or crafts, during the interview. Open-ended questions are best at eliciting responses. Complex and overly simple words should be avoided. Most children enjoy describing what they've learned but may need to be encouraged to express themselves (Fargas Malet et al. 2010, 6–9).

Focus Groups

Like interviews, focus groups are conducted in person, but with several people instead of just one-on-one. A group of six to ten participants is ideal. In our outcome scenario example, staff might want to invite parents to discuss whether the library's community garden has helped them and their children learn how to eat healthier food. Though the questions are compiled in advance, the group dynamic can take the conversation in unexpected directions. Therefore, the facilitator needs to be adept at managing people and making sure everyone has a chance to speak. Someone not participating in the discussion should be assigned to take notes. Providing incentives, such as small plants or seedlings, shows focus group attendees that the library appreciates their input.

When conducting focus groups composed of children or teens, all participants should be approximately the same age—for example, all seven- and eight-year-olds or all thirteen- and fourteen-year-olds. Do not include children and teens in the same group. As with one-on-one interviews, the facilitator may want to provide drawing materials or manipulatives, such as pipe cleaners, to help children focus. Center the discussion on the program being evaluated and how it has impacted participants: "What have you learned as a result of planting seeds in the library's garden?" "What new foods have you tasted in the garden?" "What does nature mean to you now that you've seen plants grow in the garden?" "What animals have you seen in the library's garden?" Since young people may not feel comfortable giving honest feedback to an adult they know and like, the children's librarian should refrain from leading the focus group. Older kids, however, have no such compunctions and so are usually happy to tell the teen librarian exactly how they feel (California Library Association n.d.).

Observation

Wonder what happens in the library's garden every day? The best way to find out is through observation. Sometimes called "mystery shopping," observation is an effective way of studying events and activities as they happen. Evaluators intentionally insert themselves into environments that they then carefully observe and unobtrusively record, usually via written notes, in hopes of identifying certain patterns and trends. When observing a garden, for example, you might want to visit the site several times a week, on different days and times, to get a complete snapshot of what goes on there. Visits should be long enough to see what really happens in that space: Do students quietly read to themselves, or is the garden more of a social gathering spot for young people? Do parents burst into spontaneous song or storytelling with their children? Is the garden a lunch spot for local office workers? And just how popular is that secluded bench under the sycamore tree? Observation provides a firsthand account of activity, thus creating a qualitative context for other data, such as output tallies.

Observation is also useful in evaluating program results, which, in some cases, may have to be witnessed firsthand to be fully understood. Children can tell us that they now know the importance of soil in growing plants, but seeing their excitement as they replenish the library's compost bin is a whole other level of validation. "We got to touch dirt," a fifth-grader exclaimed after making a container for worms ("Green Thumbs at Work" 2018). As an example, the Brooklyn Public Library recently asked an occupational therapist to observe and evaluate the effectiveness of one of its inclusive Garden Club programs. The therapist's detailed report included a written snapshot of all the activities that occurred during the program—for example, looking for bugs, weeding, and watering plants—as well as a comprehensive description of the visual, auditory, olfactory, tactile, proprioceptive, and vestibular elements in the surrounding environment. Several recommendations were made on how to improve the program. But, overall, the observation provided positive evidence that program participants successfully experienced "different aspects of the process of gardening"—data that could be captured only by seeing the program firsthand. (For a complete copy of the evaluator's report, see appendix D.)

SHARING RESULTS

As library professionals, we librarians are very familiar with compiling reports for governing bodies, funders, and community partners, all of whom "are looking for accountability" (Gross, Mediavilla, and Walter 2016). We may even celebrate a "successful venture" with the staff and stakeholders who helped make it happen (74). We are, however, often less adept at sharing our accomplishments with the community at large (OBPE step 5). And yet librarians in one western state recently expressed regret that residents and local officials don't know what libraries do. Their proposed solution: reach out and become more relevant to their communities.

Throughout this book, we have described many outstanding library garden programs. Some of them have received awards, but most remain unsung and, quite frankly, were often difficult to find, even on the Internet. As Jordan (2013) points out, not only do libraries fail to report the success of their garden programs, but they don't even post photos of their gardens on their websites! "A garden can be a natural part of a marketing plan," she admonishes, "and adding photos to the library's website . . . and other social media sites may help to draw the attention of people who may not otherwise be attracted to the library" (109). After all, most people are probably more familiar with gardens than they are with libraries.

Libraries should not only provide access to traditional sources of learning; they should also provide space to practice what is learned. As Jordan (2013) insists, "libraries with gardens are transmitting information in a more dynamic, physical way" (108). Children attend a storytime on healthy eating and then go outside to the Charles E. Miller Branch's Peter Rabbit patch to see how food grows (Howard County Library System 2014). Teens in El Dorado County attend a program on how to construct raised vegetable beds and then actually build several beds on library property (Amos 2015). Gardens move a library's makerspace outside.

Library gardens also provide green spaces where there were none before: a converted parking lot on Long Island; a former concrete patio in Berkeley County, South Carolina; living walls in academic libraries in Toronto and Montreal; and rooftop gardens in Austin, Vancouver, and Salt Lake City. All of these gardens inject natural beauty into the urban landscape, while helping residents connect with nature. They also, in some cases, provide food to local residents and demonstrate healthy eating. For instance, community gardens now grow in the midst of food deserts, thanks to public libraries in Sacramento and South Sioux City, Nebraska. Regardless of the type of library or its garden, the outcomes are the same: "to create a place where people find connections with each other, with their library, and with the beauty of nature all around us" (McCammond-Watts 2015).

Every library garden has a story to tell. We hope the stories in this book will inspire you to plant your own garden and share the fruits of your labor with the community.

NOTE

1. M. Giliam, personal communication, September 12, 2017.

Reading areas' hanging gardens, Reno branch, Washoe County Library, Nevada
Photo credit: Sarah and Jeff Scott

Rooftop garden at Vancouver Public Library, British Columbia, Canada
Photo credit: Vancouver Public Library

Medicinal plants at the National Library of Medicine, Washington, DC
Photo credit: Photo by Steve Greenberg; courtesy of the National Library of Medicine

Austin Public Library's central library rooftop garden, Texas
Photo credit: Patrick Y. Wong/AtelierWong.com; courtesy of Austin Public Library

David Barton Community Labyrinth and Reflective Garden, Metropolitan State University, Minnesota
Photo credit: Metropolitan State University, Tom Roster

Garden labyrinth at the Placitas Community Library, New Mexico
Photo credit: © Mike Stoy

Waterfall at Mid-Columbia Libraries' Kennewick branch demonstration gardens
Photo credit: Washington State University, Benton-Franklin Master Gardeners

Xeriscape Botanical Garden, Glendale Public Library, Arizona
Photo credit: Sharon K. Bushman

Looking down on Brown County Library's Cellcom Children's Edible Garden in Wisconsin
Photo credit: Cellcom Children's Edible Garden photo courtesy of Brown County Library, Green Bay, Wisconsin

Living wall at Centennial College's Progress Library in Ontario, Canada
Photo credit: Ania Potyrala, Photographer

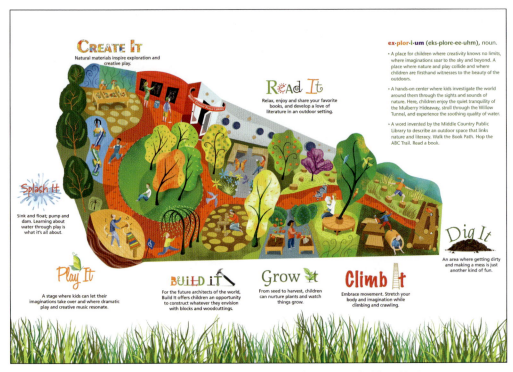

Nature Explorium at Middle Country Public Library, Centereach, New York
Photo credit: Middle Country Public Library

Albuquerque Rose Society garden, Tony Hillerman branch, Albuquerque Public Library
Photo credit: Bill Farmer

R. Howard Webster Library, Concordia University Library, Montreal, Canada
Photo credit: Adrien Williams/Concordia Library

National Institutes of Health Library garden, Washington, DC
Photo credit: Bradley Otterson

Contemplative garden at the Armstrong Browning Library, Baylor University, Texas
Photo credit: Baylor Photography

Imaginarium Garden, Southfield Public Library, Michigan
Photo credit: Don Meadows

APPENDIX A
A Tour of All the Gardens Mentioned in This Book

Entries are arranged first by continent, then by country (for North America), and finally by region and alphabetically by state (for the United States).

NORTH AMERICA
Canada

Centennial College Library
941 Progress Avenue, Scarborough, ON M1G 3V4, Canada
https://library.centennialcollege.ca/about-the-library/progress-campus
Academic Library
Living Wall (Interior)

Surrey Libraries, Semiahmoo Branch
1815 152 Street, Surrey, BC V4A 9Y9, Canada
www.surreylibraries.ca/locations/semiahmoo-library
Public Library
Living Wall (Exterior)

Vancouver Public Library, Central Library
350 West Georgia Street, Vancouver, BC V6B 6B1, Canada
www.vpl.ca
Public Library
Rooftop Garden, Reading Garden

Mexico

Biblioteca Vasconcelos
Mosqueta, Eje 1 Nte. S/N, Buenavista, 06350 Ciudad de México, CDMX, Mexico
www.bibliotecavasconcelos.gob.mx
National Library
Botanical Garden, Sustainability

United States
New England
- MASSACHUSETTS

Boston Public Library, East Boston Branch
365 South Bremen Street, Boston, MA 02128
www.bpl.org/locations/21
Public Library
Sustainability

Greenfield Community College, Nahman-Watson Library
One College Drive, Greenfield, MA 01301
www.gcc.mass.edu/library
Academic Library
Seed Library

Harvard Graduate School of Education, Gutman Library
6 Appian Way, Cambridge, MA 02138
www.gse.harvard.edu/library
Academic Library
Living Wall (Interior), Indoor Garden

Harvard University Library, Lamont Library
Harvard Yard, Cambridge, MA 02138
https://library.harvard.edu/libraries/lamont
Academic Library
Outdoor Reading Room

West Tisbury Free Public Library
1042 State Road, West Tisbury, MA 02575
www.westtisburyfreepubliclibrary.org
Public Library
Certified Wildlife Habitat

- **NEW HAMPSHIRE**

Plaistow Public Library
85 Main Street, Plaistow, NH 03865
www.plaistowlibrary.com
Public Library
Demonstration Garden

Mid-Atlantic

- **MARYLAND**

Eastern Correctional Institute (MD),
  Green Garden
30420 Revells Neck Road, Westover, MD
  21890
www.dpscs.state.md.us/locations/eci.shtml
Prison Library
Community Garden, Community Center

Howard County Library System, Charles E.
  Miller Branch and Historical Center,
  Enchanted Garden
9421 Frederick Road, Ellicott City, MD 21042
https://hclibrary.org/locations/miller-branch/
  enchanted-garden
Public Library
Native Garden, Pollinator Garden

National Institutes of Health Clinical
  Center—NIH Library
10 Center Drive, RM 1L01, Bethesda, MD
  20892
www.nihlibrary.nih.gov/agency/nih
Academic Library
Garden Reading Room, Sustainability

National Libraries of Medicine
8600 Rockville Pike, Bethesda, MD 20894
www.nlm.nih.gov
Academic Library
Medicinal Garden, Contemplative Garden

Washington County Free Library,
  Boonsboro Free Library
401 Potomac Street, Boonsboro, MD 21713
www.washcolibrary.org/?q=boonsboro
Public Library
Demonstration Garden

- **NEW JERSEY**

New Milford High School Library
330 River Road, New Milford, NJ 07646
www.newmilfordschools.org
School Library Media Center
Demonstration Garden

- **NEW YORK**

Brooklyn Public Library, Arlington Library
203 Arlington Avenue, Brooklyn, NY 11207
www.bklynlibrary.org/locations/arlington
Public Library
Landscape Garden, Reading Garden

Brooklyn Public Library, Central Library,
  Our Garden Club
10 Grand Army Plaza, Brooklyn NY 11238
www.bklynlibrary.org/locations/central
Public Library
Demonstration Garden

Brooklyn Public Library, Flatlands Library,
  Our Garden Club
2065 Flatbush Avenue, Brooklyn, NY 11234
www.bklynlibrary.org/locations/flatlands
Public Library
Inclusive Garden, Demonstration Garden

Brooklyn Public Library, Park Slope Library
431 Sixth Avenue, Brooklyn, NY 11215
www.bklynlibrary.org/locations/park-slope
Public Library
Community Center Garden, Play Garden

Brooklyn Public Library, Red Hook Library,
  Our Garden Club
8 Wolcott Street, Brooklyn, NY 11231
www.bklynlibrary.org/locations/red-hook
Public Library
Inclusive Garden, Bilingual Signage/Programs,
  Seed Exchange

Brooklyn Public Library, Sunset Park Library,
  Our Garden Club
5108 Fourth Avenue, Brooklyn, NY 11232
www.bklynlibrary.org/locations/sunset-park
Public Library
Inclusive Garden, Bilingual Signage/Programs

APPENDIX A: A Tour of All the Gardens Mentioned in This Book | 95

Middle Country Public Library,
Nature Explorium
101 Eastwood Boulevard, Centereach, NY 11720
www.mcplibrary.org/children/nature-explorium
Public Library
Children's Garden

New York Public Library, Stephen A. Schwarzman Building, *The Reading Room*
476 Fifth Avenue, New York, NY 10018
www.nypl.org/locations/schwarzman
Public Research Library
Garden Reading Room

Northern Onondaga Public Library,
Cicero Branch, *LibraryFarm*
8686 Knowledge Lane, Cicero, NY 13039
www.nopl.org/services/spaces/library-farm
Public Library
Demonstration Garden, Food Garden

Queens Library at Whitestone
151-10 14 Road, Whitestone, NY 11357
www.queenslibrary.org/Whitestone
Public Library
Landscape Garden

Queens Library, Woodhaven Library
85-41 Forest Parkway, Woodhaven, NY 11421
www.queenslibrary.org/Woodhaven
Public Library
Landscape Garden

Rikers Island Correctional Facility
11-11 Hazen Street – 18-18 Hazen Street, East Elmhurst, NY 11270
Prison Library
Demonstration Garden

Rochester Public Library
115 South Avenue, Rochester, NY 14604
https://roccitylibrary.org
Public Library
Memorial Garden

Sachem Public Library
150 Holbrook Road, Holbrook, NY 11741
www.sachemlibrary.org
Public Library
Contemplative Garden

• PENNSYLVANIA

Carnegie Library of Pittsburgh,
Squirrel Hill Branch
5801 Forbes Avenue, Pittsburgh, PA 15217
www.carnegielibrary.org/clp_location/squirrel-hill
Public Library
Demonstration Garden

Lackawanna County Library System, Albright Memorial Library
500 Vine Street, Scranton, PA 18509
http://lclshome.org/b/albright-memorial-library
Public Library
Landscape Garden

Lansdowne Public Library
55 South Lansdowne Avenue, Lansdowne, PA 19050
www.lansdownelibrary.org
Public Library
Demonstration Garden, Sustainability

Mt. Lebanon Pubic Library
16 Castle Shannon Boulevard, Pittsburgh, PA 15228
www.mtlebanonlibrary.org
Public Library
Wildlife Habitat, Rainwater Garden

• VIRGINIA

Arlington Public Library, Central Library
1015 North Quincy Street, Arlington VA 22201
https://library.arlingtonva.us/locations/central-library
Public Library
Community Garden, Demonstration Garden

APPENDIX A: A Tour of All the Gardens Mentioned in This Book

Arlington Public Library, Glencarlyn Library
300 South Kensington Street, Arlington, VA 22204
https://library.arlingtonva.us/locations/glencarlyn-branch-library
Public Library
Demonstration Garden

Arlington Public Library, Westover Branch
1644 North McKinley Road #3, Arlington, VA 23225
https://library.arlingtonva.us/locations/westover-branch-library
Public Library
Demonstration Garden

Staunton Public Library, *Brenda Lee Papke Memorial Sensory Garden*
1 Churchville Avenue, Staunton, VA 24401
www.ci.staunton.va.us/departments/library
Public Library—National Library Services for the Blind
Sensory Garden

Southeast

▪ ALABAMA

Jefferson County Library Cooperative, The Library at The Gardens
2612 Lane Park Road, Birmingham, AL 35223
www.bbgardens.org/library.php
Public Library
Botanical Garden

▪ DISTRICT OF COLUMBIA

Harvard University Library, Dumbarton Oaks: Research Library and Collection
1703 Thirty-Second Street NW, Washington, DC 20007
www.doaks.org
Academic Library
Demonstration Garden

▪ FLORIDA

Apopka Elementary School
311 Vick Road, Apopka, FL 32712
https://apopkaes.ocps.net
School Library
Demonstration Garden

Pasco County Library, New River Branch Library
34043 State Road 54, Wesley Chapel, FL 33543
www.pascolibraries.org/about-us/locations-and-hours/new-river-branch-library
Public Library
Community Center

▪ GEORGIA

Forsyth County Library, Cumming Library, *Secret Garden*
585 Dahlonega Street, Cumming GA, 30040
www.forsythpl.org/locations/hoursAndLocations.aspx?branch=cu
Public Library
Demonstration Garden, Children's Garden

Forsyth County Library, Hampton Park
5345 Settingdown Road, Cumming, GA 30041
www.forsythpl.org/locations/hoursAndLocations.aspx?branch=hp
Public Library
Pollinator Garden, Certified Wildlife Habitat

Forsyth County Library, Post Road Library, *Poetry Garden*
5010 Post Road, Cumming, GA 30040
www.forsythpl.org/locations/hoursAndLocations.aspx?branch=pr
Public Library
Demonstration Garden

Gwinnett County Public Library, Buford–Sugar Hill Branch
2100 Buford Highway, Buford, GA 30518
www.gwinnettpl.org/venue/buford-sugar-hill-branch
Public Library
Aquaponic Garden

APPENDIX A: A Tour of All the Gardens Mentioned in This Book

Gwinnett County Public Library, Centerville Branch
3025 Bethany Church Road, Snellville, GA 30039
www.gwinnettpl.org/venue/centerville-branch
Public Library
Aquaponic Garden

Gwinnett County Public Library, Collins Hill Branch
455 Camp Perrin Road NE, Lawrenceville, GA 30043
www.gwinnettpl.org/venue/collins-hill-branch
Public Library
Aquaponic Garden

Gwinnett County Public Library,
Dacula Branch
265 Dacula Road, Dacula, GA 30019
www.gwinnettpl.org/venue/dacula-branch
Public Library
Aquaponic Garden

Gwinnett County Public Library,
Duluth Branch
3480 Duluth Park Lane, Duluth, GA 30096
www.gwinnettpl.org/venue/duluth-branch
Public Library
Aquaponic Garden

Gwinnett County Public Library,
Five Forks Branch
2780 Five Forks Trickum Road, Lawrenceville, GA 30044
www.gwinnettpl.org/venue/five-forks-branch
Public Library
Aquaponic Garden

Gwinnett County Public Library,
Grayson Branch
700 Grayson Parkway, Grayson, GA 30017
www.gwinnettpl.org/venue/grayson-branch
Public Library
Aquaponic Garden

Gwinnett County Public Library,
Hamilton Mill Branch
3690 Braselton Highway, Dacula, GA 30019
www.gwinnettpl.org/venue/hamilton-mill-branch
Public Library
Aquaponic Garden

Gwinnett County Public Library,
Lawrenceville Branch
1001 Lawrenceville Highway, Lawrenceville, GA 30046
www.gwinnettpl.org/venue/lawrenceville-branch
Public Library
Aquaponic Garden

Gwinnett County Public Library,
Lilburn Branch
4817 Church Street NW, Lilburn, GA 30047
www.gwinnettpl.org/venue/lilburn-branch
Public Library
Aquaponic Garden

Gwinnett County Public Library,
Mountain Park Branch
1210 Pounds Road SW, Lilburn, GA 30047
www.gwinnettpl.org/venue/mountain-park-branch
Public Library
Aquaponic Garden

Gwinnett County Public Library, Norcross Branch
6025 Buford Highway, Norcross, GA 30071
www.gwinnettpl.org/venue/norcross-branch
Public Library
Aquaponic Garden

Gwinnett County Public Library, Peachtree Corners Branch
5570 Spalding Drive, Peachtree Corners, GA 30092
www.gwinnettpl.org/venue/peachtree-corners-branch
Public Library
Aquaponic Garden

Gwinnett County Public Library,
   Snellville Branch
2740 Lenora Church Road, Snellville, GA
   30078
www.gwinnettpl.org/venue/snellville-branch
Public Library
Aquaponic Garden

Gwinnett County Public Library,
   Suwanee Branch
361 Main Street, Suwanee, GA 30024
www.gwinnettpl.org/venue/suwanee-branch
Public Library
Aquaponic Garden

- **NORTH CAROLINA**

Eastern Carolina University,
   Laupus Library, Country Doctor Museum
7089 Peele Road, Bailey, NC 27807
www.countrydoctormuseum.org/index.cfm
Academic Library
Medicinal Garden, Historical Plant Collection

University of North Carolina,
   Health Sciences Library, *Sam W Hewitt*
   Medicinal Plant Garden
335 South Columbia Street, Chapel Hill, NC
   27599
www.hsl.unc.edu
Academic Library
Medicinal Garden

Wayne County Library, Goldsboro Library
1001 East Ash Street, Goldsboro, NC 27530
www.wcpl.org
Public Library
Community Garden

- **SOUTH CAROLINA**

The Berkeley County Library System,
   Sangaree Library, *Sangaree Community*
   Garden
595 Sangaree Parkway, Summerville, SC
   29486
https://berkeleylibrarysc.org/
   locations-and-hours/sangaree-library
Public Library
Community Garden

Lexington County Public Library, Irmo Branch
6251 St. Andrews Road, Columbia, SC 29212
www.lex.lib.sc.us
Public Library
Certified Wildlife Habitat

- **TENNESSEE**

Portland High School,
   Panther Community Garden
600 College Street, Portland, TN 37148
https://phs.sumnerschools.org
School Library Media Center
Community Garden, Community Center

Westmeade Elementary School
6641 Clearbrook Drive, Nashville, TN 37205
https://schools.mnps.org/westmeade
   -elementary-school
School Library Media Center
Demonstration Garden, Wildlife Habitat

Midwest

- **ILLINOIS**

Addison Public Library
4 Friendship Plaza, Addison, IL 60101
http://addisonlibrary.org
Public Library
Rooftop Garden

Arlington Heights Memorial Library
500 North Dunton Avenue, Arlington Heights,
   IL 60004
www.ahml.info
Public Library
Teen Garden, Demonstration Garden

Chicago Public Library,
   Harold Washington Library Center
400 South State Street, Chicago, IL 60605
www.chipublib.org/locations/34
Public Library
Indoor Garden, Seed Library

APPENDIX A: A Tour of All the Gardens Mentioned in This Book | 99

Chillicothe Public Library District
430 North Bradley Avenue, Chillicothe, IL 61523
www.chillicothepubliclibrary.org/1
Public Library
Demonstration Garden

Northlake Public Library
231 North Wolf Road, Northlake, IL 60164
www.northlakelibrary.org
Public Library
Demonstration Garden

Princeton Public Library
698 East Peru Street, Princeton, IL 61356
https://princetonpl.org
Public Library
Pollinator Garden

Stickney Forrest View Public Library District
6800 West Forty-Third Street, Stickney, IL 60402
www.sfvpld.org
Public Library
Demonstration Garden

Sycamore Public Library
103 East State Street, Sycamore, IL 60178
www.sycamorelibrary.org
Public Library
Demonstration Garden

Western Illinois University,
  Leslie F. Malpass Library
One University Circle, Macomb, IL 61455
www.wiu.edu/libraries
Academic Library
Indoor Garden

Zion-Benton Public Library
2400 Gabriel Avenue, Zion, IL 60099
https://zblibrary.info
Public Library
Demonstration Garden

• **MICHIGAN**

Grand Rapids Public Library
111 Library Street NE, Grand Rapids, MI 49503
www.grpl.org
Public Library
Sustainability

Southfield Public Library
26300 Evergreen Road, Southfield MI 48076
https://southfieldlibrary.org
Public Library
Children's Garden, Landscape Garden

Waterford Township Public Library
5168 Civic Center Drive, Waterford Township, MI 48329
www.waterfordmi.gov/477/Library
Public Library
Memorial Garden

St. Louis County Library,
  Prairie Commons Branch
915 Utz Lane, Hazelwood, MO 63042
www.slcl.org/content/prairie-commons-branch
Public Library
Pollinator Garden

• **MINNESOTA**

Metropolitan State University,
  Library and Learning Center,
  Paths of Peace Labyrinth
45 East Seventh Street, Saint Paul, MN 55106
www.metrostate.edu/library
Academic Library
Contemplative Labyrinth

Saint Paul Public Library, Sun Ray
2105 Wilson Avenue, Saint Paul MN 55119
https://sppl.org/locations/SR
Public Library
Pollinator Garden, Landscape Garden

- **MISSOURI**

St. Louis County Library, Headquarters
1640 South Lindbergh Boulevard, St. Louis, MO 63131
www.slcl.org/content/headquarters
Public Library
Pollinator Garden

- **NEBRASKA**

Omaha Public Library,
   Benson Branch, *Common Soil Seed Library*
6015 Binney Street, Omaha, NE 68104
https://omahalibrary.org/locations/OB
Public Library
Seed Library

South Sioux City Public Library
2121 Dakota Avenue, South Sioux City, NE 68776
www.siouxcitylibrary.org
Public Library
Seed Library, Community Garden

- **WISCONSIN**

Brown County Library,
   Cellcom Children's Edible Garden
515 Pine Street, Green Bay, WI 54301
www.browncountylibrary.org
Public Library
Children's Garden

La Crosse Public Library
800 Main Street, La Crosse, WI 54601
www.lacrosselibrary.org
Public Library
Seed Library

Madison Public Library, Central Library
201 West Mifflin Street, Madison, WI 53703
www.madisonpubliclibrary.org
Public Library
Green Roof, Sustainability

Rosemary Garfoot Public Library
2107 Julius Street, Cross Plains, WI 53528
www.rgpl.org
Public Library
Demonstration Garden, Sustainability

Plains States

- **KANSAS**

Finney County Public Library
605 East Walnut Street, Garden City, KS 67846
http://finneylibrary.org
Public Library
Demonstration Garden

Mountain States

- **COLORADO**

Anythink, Commerce City
7185 Monaco Street, Commerce City, CO 80022
www.anythinklibraries.org/location/anythink-commerce-city
Public Library
Community Garden

Anythink, Wright Farms
5877 East 120th Avenue, Thornton, CO 80602
www.anythinklibraries.org/location/anythink-wright-farms
Public Library
Community Garden

Anythink, York Street
8990 York Street, Suite A, Thornton, CO 80229
www.anythinklibraries.org/location/anythink-york-street
Public Library
Community Garden

- **WYOMING**

Laramie County Library, Cheyenne
2200 Pioneer Avenue, Cheyenne, WY 82001
https://lclsonline.org
Public Library
Certified Wildlife Habitat, Seed Library

Northwest

ALASKA

John Trigg Ester Library
3629 Main Street, Ester, AK 99725
www.esterlibrary.org
Subscription Library
Seed Exchange

WASHINGTON

Daffodil Elementary School Library
1509 Valley Avenue E, Sumner, WA 98390
www.sumnersd.org/domain/1312
School Library Media Center
Demonstration Garden

Mid-Columbia Libraries, Kennewick Branch
1620 South Union Street, Kennewick, WA 99338
www.midcolumbialibraries.org/branches/kennewick
Public Library
Demonstration Garden

Sno-Isle Libraries, Mukilteo Library
4675 Harbour Pointe Boulevard, Mukilteo, WA 98275
www.sno-isle.org/locations/mukilteo
Public Library
Certified Wildlife Habitat

Southwest

ARIZONA

Davis Bilingual Elementary Magnet School
500 West St. Mary's Road, Tucson, AZ 85701
http://tusd1.org/davis
School Library Media Center
Aquaponic Garden, Bilingual Signage/Programs

Glendale Public Library,
   Main Library, *Xeriscape Botanical Garden*
5959 West Brown Street, Glendale, AZ 85302
http://web.gccaz.edu/glendalelibrary
Public Library
Botanical Garden

NEW MEXICO

Placitas Community Library
453 Highway 165, Placitas, NM 87043
http://placitaslibrary.com
Public Library
Labyrinth, Contemplative Garden

**The Public Library, Albuquerque and
   Bernalillo County,** Tony Hillerman Library
8205 Apache NE, Albuquerque, NM 87110
https://abqlibrary.org/tonyhillerman
Public Library
Rose Garden

TEXAS

Austin Public Library, Central Library
710 West César Chávez Street, Austin, TX 78701
http://library.austintexas.gov
Public Library
Rooftop Garden, Native Plants

Baylor University,
   Armstrong Browning Library and Museum
710 Speight Avenue, Waco, TX 76706
www.baylor.edu/browninglibrary/index.php?id=942418
Academic Library
Contemplative Garden

Marcia R. Garza Elementary School
810 East El Gato Road, Alamo, TX 78516
www.psjaisd.us/garza
School Library Media Center
Aquaponic Garden

San Antonio Public Library, Landa Library
233 Bushnell, San Antonio, TX 78212
www.mysapl.org/Visit/Locations/Landa-Library
Public Library
Demonstration Garden, Native Plant Garden

Westbank Libraries,
   Westbank Community Garden
1309 Westbank Drive, Austin, TX 78746
www.westbanklibrary.com/community-garden
Public Library
Community Garden

West

▪ CALIFORNIA

Chula Vista Public Library
365 F Street, Chula Vista, CA 91910
www.chulavistaca.gov/library
Public Library
Native Plant Garden

Felton Library and Nature Discovery Park
[under construction]
Public Library
Native Plant Garden, Demonstration Garden

Hall Middle School
200 Doherty Drive, Larkspur, CA 94939
www.lcmschools.org/Hall
School Library Media Center
Seed Library

Huntington Beach Public Library, Central Library
7111 Talbert Avenue, Huntington Beach, CA 92648
www.hbpl.org
Public Library
Indoor Garden

Long Beach Public Library, Michelle Obama Neighborhood Library, *Learning Garden*
5870 Atlantic Avenue, Long Beach, CA 90805
www.lbpl.org/locations/michelle_obama/default.asp
Public Library
Demonstration Garden

Los Angeles Public Library, Central Library
630 West Fifth Street, Los Angeles, CA 90071
www.lapl.org
Public Library
Landscape Garden

Marin County Free Library, Civic Center Library
3501 Civic Center Drive, Room 427, San Rafael, CA 94903
www.marinlibrary.org/civic-center
Public Library
Indoor Garden

Mill Valley Public Library
375 Throckmorton Avenue, Mill Valley, CA 94941
www.millvalleylibrary.org
Public Library
Demonstration Garden, Sustainability

Oakland Public Library, César E. Chávez Branch
3301 East Twelfth Street, Suite 271, Oakland, CA 94601
http://oaklandlibrary.org/locations/cesar-e-chavez-branch
Public Library
Demonstration Garden, Seed Library, Bilingual Signage/Programs

Oakland Public Library, Temescal Branch
5205 Telegraph Avenue, Oakland, CA 94609
http://oaklandlibrary.org/locations/temescal-branch
Public Library
Tool Lending Library

Pauma AA'Alivikat Library
1010 Reservation Road, Pauma Valley, CA 92061
www.paumatribe.com/pauma-community/pauma-library
Tribal Library
Demonstration Garden

Richmond Public Library, *Richmond Grows Seed Lending Library*
325 Civic Center Plaza, Richmond, CA 94804
www.richmondgrowsseeds.org
Public Library
Seed Library

Sacramento Public Library, Colonial Heights
4799 Stockton Boulevard, Sacramento, CA 95820
www.saclibrary.org/Locations/Colonial-Heights
Public Library
Native Plant Garden

APPENDIX A: A Tour of All the Gardens Mentioned in This Book | 103

Sacramento Public Library, Rancho Cordova
9845 Folsom Boulevard, Sacramento, CA 95827
www.saclibrary.org/Locations/Rancho-Cordova
Public Library
Demonstration Garden

San Bernardino County Library,
    Highland Sam J. Racadio Library & Environmental Learning Center
7863 Central Avenue, Highland, CA 92346
www.sbclib.org/LibraryLocations/Highland SamJRacadioLibrary.aspx
Public Library
Rooftop Garden, Sustainability

San Francisco Public Library, Mission Branch
300 Bartlett Street, San Francisco, CA 94110
https://sfpl.org/?pg=0100000201
Public Library
Demonstration Garden

San Mateo County Libraries, Pacifica Sanchez
1111 Terra Nova Boulevard, Pacifica, CA 94044
https://smcl.org/locations/1Z
Public Library
Demonstration Garden, Garden Reading Room

Santa Clara County Library, Cupertino Library
10800 Torre Avenue, Cupertino, CA 95014
www.sccl.org/Locations/Cupertino
Public Library
Children's Garden, Teen Demonstration Garden

Solano County Library,
    Fairfield Civic Center Library
1150 Kentucky Street, Fairfield, CA 94533
www.solanolibrary.com/fairfield-civic-center
Public Library
Memorial Garden

St. Helena Pubic Library
1492 Library Lane, St. Helena, CA 94574
www.shpl.org
Public Library
Vineyard

▪ **HAWAII**

Mānoa Elementary School,
    The Reading-Peace Garden
3155 Mānoa Road, Honolulu, HI 96822
www.manoaschool.com/library-corner.html
School Library Media Center
Outdoor Reading Room

▪ **NEVADA**

Washoe County Library System,
    Downtown Reno Library
301 South Center Street, Reno, NV 89501
www.washoecountylibrary.us/libraries/downtown-reno.php
Public Library
Indoor Garden

▪ **UTAH**

Salt Lake City Public Library, Main Library
210 East 400 South, Salt Lake City, UT 84111
www.slcpl.org
Public Library
Rooftop Garden, Sustainability

University of Utah, J. Willard Marriott Library
295 South 1500 East, Salt Lake City, UT 84112
www.lib.utah.edu
Academic Library
Sustainability, Green Roof

SOUTH AMERICA

Biblioteca Nacional de Chile
Libertador Bernardo O'Higgins 651, Santiago, Chile
www.bibliotecanacional.cl/sitio
National Library
Outdoor Reading Room

ASIA

National Library Singapore
100 Victoria Street, Singapore 188064
www.nlb.gov.sg
National Library
Rooftop Garden, Sustainability

AUSTRALIA

Green Square Library
355 Botany Road, Zetland NSW 2017, Australia
www.cityofsydney.nsw.gov.au/explore/libraries/locations/green-square?utm_source=google&utm
    _medium=organic&utm_content=greensquarelibrary&utm_campaign=googlemybusiness
Public Library
Community Center

AFRICA

Cheetah Conservation Fund
International Research and Education Centre, outside of Otjiwarongo, Namibia
http://cheetah.org/2013/06/a-garden-for-cheetahs
Research Library
Seed Library

Robben Island Prison
Robben Island, Cape Town 7400, South Africa
Prison Library
Demonstration Garden, Contemplative Garden

EUROPE

Françoise-Mitterand Library
Quai François Mauriac, 75706 Paris, France
www.bnf.fr/fr/acc/x.accueil.html
National Library
Internal Forest Garden

Rheinland-Pflaz Library, Kaiserslautern Family and MWR
Landstuhl, Germany
https://kaiserslautern.armymwr.com/programs/rheinland-pfalz-library
U.S. Army Morale, Welfare & Recreation Libraries/U.S. Military Installation
Outdoor Reading Room

APPENDIX B
Sample Community Garden Rules, Regulations, and Gardener Agreements
Northern Onondaga Public Library

The mission of the LibraryFarm is to provide a place for the community to grow, share, and learn about food literacy and organic, sustainable gardening.

General Information

The LibraryFarm is an organic, educational garden located on the grounds of the Northern Onondaga Public Library (NOPL) at Cicero. Its operation is overseen by the NOPL Cicero Library and the LibraryFarm Steering Committee, which is made up of LibraryFarm gardeners.

All LibraryFarm gardeners agree to use organic methods at all times. No fertilizers will be used in the garden unless they are certified organic.

The LibraryFarm has individual garden beds as well as designated food pantry beds. Individual beds are tended by an assigned gardener(s). All produce from the individual beds can be used or donated to the pantries by the assigned gardener. The food pantry beds are taken care of by members of the Food Pantry Team, and all produce is weighed and then delivered to local food pantries by volunteers.

All new and returning gardeners must sign the Liability Release and Community Agreement every year that they wish to participate in the LibraryFarm. These documents need to be turned in to the NOPL Cicero Library. Gardeners must be over 18 years old or be signed up to garden with an adult.

Garden Bed Assignments

The NOPL Cicero Library reserves the right to shift, move, or make other necessary garden bed/plot modifications within the LibraryFarm.

Returning Gardeners
Gardeners can continue using the same garden bed each year by completing the Community Agreement and Liability Waiver and returning it to the NOPL Cicero Library by the *March 15th* deadline. If paperwork is not received by this deadline, garden beds may be reassigned to new gardeners from the waitlist.

New Gardeners

Gardeners interested in joining the LibraryFarm program can sign up beginning November 1 to get on the Garden Waitlist for the following growing season. Each spring as new garden beds become available, gardeners from the waitlist will be contacted. New gardeners will need to turn in a signed Community Agreement and Liability Release before being assigned a vacant plot.

Extra Garden Beds/Plots

Gardeners will all be assigned one raised bed or in-ground garden plot to start. If additional beds/plots are available after the Garden Waitlist has been emptied, second plots may be assigned to those interested on a first come, first served basis. Second plots are not necessarily renewable from year to year and will only be assigned if there is a surplus of garden beds available.

Abandoned Garden Beds/Plots

During the growing season (April to October), abandoned gardens will be reassigned as second plots or given to new gardeners from the Garden Waitlist. Throughout the growing season, a plot very overgrown with weeds and appearing unplanted or untended will be considered abandoned and revert to NOPL Cicero Library custodianship, unless the status of the plot has been discussed with the LibraryFarm representatives and exceptions are made. The LibraryFarm will make no more than three attempts to notify gardeners in advance.

Garden Maintenance and Expectations

Gardeners will be expected to actively maintain their plot from *June 1st* through *November 1st*. This includes the garden plot, the walkways or paths, and other areas adjacent to their plots. Gardeners are expected to plant, maintain, weed, harvest, and clean up.

Till-by and Plant-by Dates

All plots must be turned or tilled by *June 1st*. If a plot has not been turned over by this date, it will be immediately considered abandoned and reassigned. The planting deadline is *June 15th*. Gardeners who cannot plant by this date must notify the LibraryFarm *beforehand* to discuss an arrangement. Otherwise, plots not planted will be considered abandoned and reassigned.

End of Season

The LibraryFarm gardening season ends on *November 1st,* and all annual vegetation, including empty stalks, trellises, garden tools, signs, debris, and stakes must be removed by that date. This date applies equally to new gardens as well as renewals. The only exception will be winter crops and the numbered plot signs, which may remain in the plot.

Vacations and Leaves of Absence

Vacations and absences are normal, and gardeners are encouraged to tell the LibraryFarm as soon as possible in order to make housekeeping arrangements with neighbors or with the Helping Hands Team.

Communication

Gardeners are responsible for maintaining a viable means of communicating with the LibraryFarm. E-mail is the primary means of LibraryFarm communications. Another means for communication is the LibraryFarm Facebook page. Those who choose to communicate through Facebook are requested to keep conversations friendly and supportive, and to not represent the opinions of other gardeners, the NOPL Cicero Library, or the LibraryFarm in their conversations.

Public Education

Gardeners are requested to participate in garden tours and impromptu learning and sharing that take place in the LibraryFarm throughout the growing season. Gardeners are also asked to participate in the creation of garden literature, including production of "stake stories" that will describe plot contents, aspirations, experiences, or thoughts for each garden; unique creativity is strongly encouraged.

Miscellaneous LibraryFarm Rules
- Avoid growing plants or trellises higher than 4 feet or gardening in manner that might block the sun or the rain from reaching a neighbor's plot.
- Prevent weed growth over 12 inches.
- Remove fallen or trimmed vegetation quickly and add to the designated compost bins.
- Remove and trash (not compost) any diseased plants.
- Avoid large plants, invasive or insidious plants, as well as most perennials.
- Never weed, trim, or harvest produce from another person's garden without consent.
- Do not drive through the garden area or perimeter without permission.
- Pets are not permitted in the LibraryFarm.

Resources

The NOPL Cicero Library will provide the LibraryFarm members with property, water, serve as a conduit for information and communication, and hold meetings and programs related to the LibraryFarm. The NOPL Cicero Library also oversees maintenance of the area, including mowing of the perimeters of the garden.

Tools and Supplies

Tools and supplies including yard bags, garbage bags, a wheelbarrow, shovels, and rakes are located in the LibraryFarm shed currently located in the rear of the south side parking lot. The key to the shed is available for checkout at the circulation desk. Personal tools as well as buckets, tarps, and bags should not be left unattended or unanchored in the garden. Containers should not be left to collect water in a manner that would attract mosquitoes.

OCCRA Compost

The NOPL Cicero Library will annually make arrangements for organic compost and mulch delivery from the Onondaga County Resource Recovery Agency (OCCRA) compost sites for use only in the LibraryFarm.

Fees and Funds

There are no fees associated with LibraryFarm. However, if the group chooses to do so, donations might be collected by the group, or by approved fundraisers to support group purchases, tools, or deliveries.

Steering Committee and Teams

LibraryFarm Steering Committee

This committee will help determine the rules of the LibraryFarm, make decisions, and coordinate activities and communications. The Steering Committee meets regularly during the year, at minimum every other month.

Food Pantry Garden Team

This team dedicates their time to grow, harvest, weigh, and deliver fresh produce to the local food pantries using the dedicated Food Pantry garden beds/plots.

Helping Hands Team

This team will help coordinate the temporary maintenance of another person's garden when such help is requested.

Open House Team

This team will organize and help facilitate the LibraryFarm annual open house(s).

Important Dates to Remember

March 15th   Community Agreement and Liability Waiver Due (returning gardeners)
April 1st   Plot Assignments Posted for New Gardeners
June 1st   Till-by Date
June 15th   Plant-by Date
November 1st End of LibraryFarm Season

For the most updated information on LibraryFarm programs, events, and workdays, please visit our website at www.nopl.org

Questions? Please give us a call at 315-699-2032

2018 LibraryFarm Liability Release and Community Agreement

I, _____, understand and agree that in consideration for access to and the use of space in the LibraryFarm owned by Northern Onondaga Public Library (NOPL), I assume any and all risk with respect to access and use of the LibraryFarm.

I acknowledge that use of the LibraryFarm exposes me to the risk of personal injury. I desire to use the LibraryFarm and agree to not hold NOPL, its officers, agents, employees, and volunteers responsible for damage or personal injury I sustain by my use of the LibraryFarm.

I expressly acknowledge that I have no known medical conditions that would prohibit me from using the LibraryFarm, and I have no known medical conditions that could increase my risk of injury while using the LibraryFarm.

By agreeing to participate in the LibraryFarm program at NOPL Cicero Library, I also agree to the following:

1. I agree to adhere to and support the LibraryFarm Rules and Responsibilities and to participate in LibraryFarm communications, work teams, and LibraryFarm events to the best of my ability.
2. I agree to not use chemical fertilizers, pesticides, or herbicides in the LibraryFarm. Seedlings obtained from inorganic growers are allowed, but once transplanted into the LibraryFarm, I will adhere to organic growing practices.
3. I agree to share my contact information (phone number and e-mail address) with NOPL Cicero Library. I also agree that it is my responsibility to keep the LibraryFarm advised of any change in my contact information.
4. I agree that any use of LibraryFarm and the LibraryFarm shed is my choice and I am responsible for personal items stored there. I will not hold the Library liable for any missing or damaged goods.
5. I agree that my use of the any tools in the shed or belonging to the LibraryFarm will be used at my own risk. In particular regarding the use of the weed trimmer, I agree to wear goggles, long sleeves, and long pants, and read and follow the safety instructions.

Name: _____

Phone: _____

E-mail Address: _____

Raised Bed/Plot # _____ *(Renewals only, new members leave blank)*

Signature: _____ Date: _____

Please sign and return this form to the NOPL at Cicero Library
8686 Knowledge Lane, Cicero, NY 13039

APPENDIX C
Sample Volunteer Gardener Application

Westbank Community Garden

Garden Agreement

April 2018

Name: _____ Date: _____

Address: _____

E-mail: _____ Library Card #: _____

Phone #: _____

A deposit of $100 is required at the time of plot assignment for full-sized plots. Deposits for smaller plots are $50. The deposit will be returned when the gardener decides to not continue with his/her plot rental and then removes all plant material from the plot.

Garden rights may be terminated for failure to pay rental fee, failure to maintain garden plot, or repeated violation of any of the below rules.

Under the honor system, every gardener is expected to volunteer *10 service hours per rental year* toward general maintenance, communal garden projects, or other tasks *beyond maintenance on one's own plot.*

I have read and agree to the Community Garden rules and I understand that failure to meet the guidelines will result in loss of gardening privileges. I understand that I am gardening at my own risk.

_____
Participant's Signature

_____
Garden Coordinator's Signature   Date

FOR COORDINATOR USE ONLY

Start date: _____

Deposit paid: _____

Plot #: _____

The Westbank Community Garden (the Garden) is an entity of the Westbank Community Library District (the Library).

General Rules
1. The Garden is organic. Artificial herbicides, insecticides, fungicides, and chemical fertilizers are not permitted. Organic fertilizers and amendments are acceptable.
2. Individual gardeners must be current library members in good standing.
3. Gardeners are responsible for the overall maintenance and appearance of their own plot and communally for the maintenance of the garden as a whole.
4. To ensure plot maintenance, gardeners must *visit the garden at least every 3 weeks* (preferably more often). There is a Visit Sheet in the shed that should be signed at every visit. If a gardener has not visited within 3 weeks, the Coordinator will issue a written warning.
5. Gardeners may arrange for other gardeners to temporarily maintain their plot. In these situations, the gardener should, for example, mark the Visit Sheet "Jane Doe on behalf of John Smith."
6. A single full-sized plot requires a $100 deposit. ($50 for smaller plots.) Deposits are to be paid for when the plot is assigned. Deposits can be paid by check to Westbank Community Garden or by credit card. For gardeners who started gardening under the annual fee model, the $25 deposit they paid will be the amount they are given back.
7. If a gardener decides to leave the garden, she/he is responsible for clearing the plots of all plant material and removing all personal items *within 14 days of notification to the coordinator or else the deposit is forfeited.* Only after the plot is completely cleared will the deposit be returned.
8. Gardeners may grow plants up the fence, so long as the plants do not overgrow horizontally beyond the plot boundary and the vines are cleared when the garden plot is vacated.
9. Keeping all grass trimmed, edging and weeding are the responsibility of the gardeners. A cordless weed whacker is kept in the shed for all to use. Please wear long pants and eye protection when weed whacking.
10. Weeds should be either (1) bagged in the paper yard bags kept in the shed and then either taken home, if your neighborhood has yard trimming pickup, or left in the garden for another gardener or Alex to take home for pickup OR (2) bagged and thrown away in the library dumpster. Please do not add weeds to the compost bins.
11. Any tools in the communal areas of the shed are for the use by gardeners. Please return tools to the shed dry and clean after use. Each gardener is assigned a shed bin for storing personal items.

12. Each gardener is required to work at least ten (10) service hours per year doing communal tasks outside of his/her plot maintenance (edging grass, tidying shed, helping organize social events, turning compost, special projects, contributing newsletter articles, etc.). In keeping with the spirit of a community garden, regular participation, enthusiasm, and sharing of knowledge are encouraged in order for the garden to thrive.
13. Gardeners are free to work on their plots at any time of the day, regardless of whether the library is open. The garden gates and tool shed will remain locked and all renters will be given an access code (the same code for both gates and the shed) by the garden coordinator. The Garden has no exterior lighting and gardeners choose to work at their own risk.
14. In case of damage sustained to the garden infrastructure, gardener may be held responsible for cost of the repair.
15. Garden rights may be terminated for failure to maintain garden plot or repeated violation of any of these rules. This is made by the Coordinator following a written warning.
16. The Garden Coordinator reserves the right to modify this agreement at any time. If there is a change, an e-mail will be sent of the changes.
17. Gardeners MAY NOT park in the staff parking lot during weekday library hours, including the hour before opening. Gardeners MAY park in the staff lot on weekdays within two hours before closing, 5–7 p.m. Monday-Thursday, and all day during the weekend. Gardeners MAY ALWAYS park in the two spots in the grass adjacent to the garden, in the visitors lot, or on neighboring streets such as Moon River Dr.
18. There is a beehive behind the locked wooden gate at the far end of the garden. Alex Meyers is the first point of contact for the hive. Contact her with any bee-related issues or if you would like to arrange to accompany her on a hive inspection.

Communications
- Alex Meyers is the Library's Garden Coordinator. For non-urgent matters, contact her at her e-mail. For urgent matters, contact her via her cell number. (Listed in the shed.)
- The Garden Coordinator will communicate with all gardeners via (1) a monthly newsletter that will be e-mailed to gardeners and posted on the library's website and (2) e-mails sent to the gardeners' listserv. This e-mail group is the best way for gardeners to communicate with each other as well.
- We have been holding Garden Get-Together potlucks twice a year on a weekday afternoon.
- It is up to each gardener to ensure that the Coordinator has his/her correct e-mail address, mailing address, and phone number.

APPENDIX D
Sample Evaluation Report

Occupational Therapy Environment and Program Evaluation

Date: 8.8.18
Branch: Central Library
Program Name: Garden Club

Description of Program
Leader greeted participants, read one story, moved bodies to gardening movements, read another story, then group completed gardening activities (looking for bugs, weeding, and watering). An alternative activity, a bug matching game, was also offered during the looking-for-bug activity.

Patrons Who Attended Program (Ages, Families, Siblings, General Needs)
12 participants ranging in age from infant to elementary age. The one infant was a sibling and most children fell within the 5–8-year-old age group. All participants were able to use the materials without further adaptations. None of the participants required adaptive seated.

Sensory Environment

Vision
The program took place in the garden of central library. There was outside light, plants, bugs, but no other visible distractors, such as moving objects, displays, etc. All participants were in view of the leader of the group arranged in a semicircle. The visual schedule had recently gone missing, so the leader provided a verbal overview of the schedule.

Auditory
Due to the location of the garden, there was traffic going by outside. A loud ambulance siren did go by during the storytime. [The leader] stopped reading and waited. It's also a good time to tell participants that there are noise-canceling headphones or they can cover their ears. Also let them know that the book was stopped until the siren passed.

Olfactory
Some olfactory sensations in the garden related to the plants and dirt, but no overwhelming fertilizer or other smells present in the garden area.

Tactile
Materials used during the program included a book, shovel, magnifying glass, bug matching game, watering cans, garden gloves. The garden gloves were tight and difficult for some participants to put on. All participants tolerated using the shovel to dig and the watering can to water. Participants did not demonstrate tactile defensiveness, and having access to the gloves and tools to interact with the garden is an important component.

Proprioceptive/Vestibular
All participants were invited to sit or stand. The seats the program typically used were missing that day so the participants did need to sit on the floor. Some supportive pillows or seats may need to be used if a participant had difficulty sitting unsupported on the ground. The gardening movements and the occupation of gardening allowed the students multiple opportunities to move into different positions, and gain proprioceptive input through joints by carrying and refilling the watering cans, digging in the dirt, and weeding.

UDL Guidelines
The program adhered to many UDL guidelines. [The leader] was able to provide multiple means of engagement and action and expression. She made sure to highlight and relate the story to the students in the group. In order to provide multiple means of representation, incorporate alternative means of auditory information by pointing to pictures in the book or using a kinesthetic movement to exemplify a part of the vocabulary. The garden program fostered a sense of collaboration and community as participants were able to work together to complete many of the activities, including gardening.

Other Comments
Gardening club at the library provides access to meaningful occupations where participants can participate with different aspects of the process of gardening.

Recommendations
- Use techniques that engage participants during storytime; allow for multiple means of expression. Some participants may have difficulty taking information in solely from listening to the story. They may need to have certain vocabulary pointed out in the book's pictures or even demonstrated with a kinesthetic movement.
- Create a visual schedule that can be displayed in large pictures behind the leader to reference.
- Make clear transitions between each activity. Provide warnings that each activity is ending, regroup, and then transition to next activity.
- Have materials that are available for sensory storytime also available during the program (fidgets, headphones, caps). At each introduction to the group, mention that there are sensory tools available if there is too loud of a sound, the lights are too bright, or if they need something to do with their hands during the storytime.

Stating these tools at the beginning makes participants more aware that they have the ability to advocate for their sensory needs and also teaches that these tools are okay and available.
- When incorporating movement into your program, some students need an adult model and a visual. If you use the garden movements frequently during this group, then consider having a visual for each exercise presented during the group.

BROOKLYN PUBLIC LIBRARY

BIBLIOGRAPHY

Albuquerque Rose Society. "Rose Garden." AlbuquerqueRose.com, 2017. www.albuquerquerose.com/rose-gallery.

Allegra, Antonia. "Barney's Backyard." SHPL.org, n.d. www.shpl.org/faq/about/barneys-backyard.

Alliance for the Arts. "Bryant Park Reading Room." In *NYC-Arts: The Complete Guide*. NYC-ARTS.org, 2015. www.nyc-arts.org/organizations/22215/bryant-park-reading-room.

American Horticultural Society (AHS). "AHS Plant Heat Zone Map: What Are Heat Zones?" AHSGardening.org, 2018. http://ahsgardening.org/gardening-resources/gardening-maps/heat-zone-map.

American Nutrition Association. "USDA Defines Food Deserts." *Nutrition Digest* 38, no. 2 (2010). http://americannutritionassociation.org/newsletter/usda-defines-food-deserts.

Amos, Jeanne. "California State Library FY 2014/2015 Library Services and Technology Act Final Program Narrative Report: Growing Teens: Community Garden." [Placerville, CA: El Dorado County Library], 2015.

Andrewes, William J. H. "Hidden Spaces: Secret Garden." *The Harvard Gazette*, September 2, 2014. https://news.harvard.edu/gazette/story/2014/09/secret-garden.

Anest, Eric. "Highland Sam J. Racadio Library and Environmental Learning Center: Practicing and Teaching Sustainability." *Salas O'Brien News*, June 21, 2018. http://news.salasobrien.com/-library-practices-and-teaches-sustainability.

Aronson, Brittany, and Judson Laughter. "The Theory and Practice of Culturally Relevant Education: A Synthesis of Research across Content Areas." *Review of Educational Research* 86, no. 1 (2016): 163–206.

Association of American Seed Control Officials (AASCO). *Recommended Uniform State Seed Law (RUSSL)*. SeedControl.org, 2016. www.seedcontrol.org/pdf/russl_2017.pdf.

Austen, Verna. "The STEM Garden." *Public Libraries Online*, January 27, 2016. http://publiclibrariesonline.org/2016/01/the-stem-garden.

Baek, John Y. "The Accidental STEM Librarian: An Exploratory Interview with Eight Librarians." National Center for Interactive Learning Education/Research Report. Boulder, CO: Space Science Institute, October 2013. www.nc4il.org/images/papers/Baek_The%20Accidental%20STEM%20Librarian.pdf.

Ban Ki-Moon, UN Secretary-General. "Nelson Mandela Once Said His Garden in Prison Gave Him Small Taste of Freedom, Recalls Secretary-General at Commemorative Public Service Event." United Nations Press Release, July 18, 2014. www.un.org/press/en/2014/sgsm16040.doc.htm.

Banks, Carrie S. "Volunteers with Disabilities: How to Make It Work." In *Library Volunteers Welcome! Strategies for Attracting, Retaining and Making the Most of Willing Helpers*, edited by Carol Smallwood and Laura Sanborn, 204–12. Jefferson, NC: McFarland, 2016.

Banks, Marcus. "Preserving the Vintage." *American Libraries*, March 1, 2017. https://americanlibrariesmagazine.org/2017/03/01/preserving-vintage-wine-libraries.

Becker, Patti Clayton. *Books and Libraries in American Society during World War II: Weapons in the War of Ideas*. New York: Routledge, 2005.

Berezowitz, Claire K., Andrea B. Bontrager Yoder, and Dale A. Schoeller. "School Gardens Enhance Academic Performance and Dietary Outcomes in Children." *Journal of School Health* 85, no. 8 (2015): 508–18. http://pdfs.semanticscholar.org/3ffc/b1cf8ddc37efae69b7b570e1cd79fe0aca2d.pdf.

Berkeley County Library System (BCLS). "The Community Garden Springs in Sangaree." BerkeleyLibrarySC.org, n.d. https://berkeleylibrarysc.org/the-community-garden-springs-in-sangaree.

Bernard, Murrye. "Centennial College Library and Academic Facility." *Contract*, March 13, 2012. www.contractdesign.com/projects/education/centennial-college-library-and-academic-facility.

Berry, John N., III. "Where Democracy Happens." *Library Journal* (June 15): 32–35.

Bibliothèque nationale de France (BNF). "Visite virtuelle site François-Mitterand." Video. Paris, France: BNF, n.d. http://multimedia.bnf.fr/visitefmitterrand.

Biel, Lindsey, and Nancy Peske. *Raising a Sensory Smart Child: The Definitive Handbook for Helping Your Child with Sensory Processing Issues*. New York: Penguin Books, 2018.

Bradley, Darren. "Neutra's Brutalist Library." *Modernist Architecture*, July 31, 2016. http://modernistarchitecture.blogspot.com/2016/07/neutras-brutalist-library_31.html.

Braun, Linda W. "The Lowdown on STEM." *American Libraries*, September 20, 2011. https://americanlibrariesmagazine.org/2011/09/20/the-lowdown-on-stem.

Brenner, Anji. "California State Library FY 2014/2015 Library Services and Technology Act Final Program Narrative Report: SmartGarden at the Mill Valley Public Library." [Mill Valley, CA: Mill Valley Public Library], 2015. www.library.ca.gov/Content/pdf/grantpdf/narrative-report/40-8427_NAR2.pdf.

Brewer, Natalie. *The Enchanted Garden Field Guide*. Columbia, MD: Howard County Library System, 2014. https://issuu.com/hoco_library/docs/eg-fieldguide4issuu.

Broderick, Pauline, and Peter Jordan, eds. *The Three Sisters: Renewing the World*. Winnepeg, Manitoba: Birch Bark Productions, 2017. http://newworldideas.ca/wp-content/uploads/2017/10/2017-Three-Sisters-Final.pdf.

Brown County Library. "Cellcom Childrens Edible Garden 2015 @ Brown County Library." YouTube video, published December 22, 2015. www.youtube.com/watch?v=fK-9VMmwwJ8.

Buffum, Richard. "Lodestar Library." *Los Angeles Times*, March 18, 1975. www.huntingtonbeachca.gov/files/users/library/complete/071004-3.pdf.

Bunting, Eve. *Flower Garden*. San Diego: Harcourt Brace, 1994.

"Calif. Contributes $1M for Felton Library, Park." *Scotts Valley Patch*, July 2, 2018. https://patch.com/california/scottsvalley/calif-contributes-1m-felton-library-park.

California Library Association. "Focus Groups." Summer at Your Library: Explore, Learn, Read, Connect, n.d. https://calchallenge.org/evaluation/outcomes/focus-groups.

Carle, Eric. *The Tiny Seed*. New York: Simon and Schuster, 2009.

———. *The Very Hungry Caterpillar*. New York: Philomel Books, 1994.

CAST. "Universal Design for Learning Guidelines," Version 2.2. CAST.org, 2018. http://udlguidelines.cast.org.

Central Docents. "Sculptor Jud Fine Reflects on the Maguire Gardens' SPINE." *LAPL Blog*, January 4, 2016. www.lapl.org/collections-resources/blogs/lapl/sculptor-jud-fine-reflects-maguire-gardens%E2%80%99-spine.

Central Minnesota Libraries Exchange (CMLE). "Episode Eight: Library Gardens." In *Linking Our Libraries* (podcast). CMLE.org, n.d. https://cmle.org/cmle-created-resources/cmle-podcast/episode-eight-library-gardens.

Central New York Community Foundation. "Northern Onondaga Public Library Grows a Greener Community with Its LibraryFarm Program." *Central New York Community Foundation NEWS*, December 11, 2015. https://cnycfblog.org/2015/12/11/library-farm.

Chamberlin, Juli, Yassi Eskandari-Qajar, and Janelle Orsi. "Planning and Zoning." UrbanAgLaw.Org, n.d. www.urbanaglaw.org/planning-and-zoning.

Chan, Kenneth. "Vancouver Public Library's Massive New Rooftop Garden to Open in the Fall." *Daily Hive*, June 6, 2018. http://dailyhive.com/vancouver/vancouver-public-library-expansion-opening-september-2018.

Children & Nature Network (C&NN). "Sun Ray Natural Library Project Launches June 12 and 13 at Sun Ray Library and Conway Park." C&NN, June 8, 2015. www.childrenandnature.org/2015/06/08/sun-ray-natural-library-project-launches-june-12-and-13-at-sun-ray-library-and-conway-park.

Chileapart.com. "National Library of Santiago Chile." News, April 8. www.chileapart.com/2014/04/08/la-biblioteca-nacional-en-santiago-de-chile/?lang=en.

City of Huntington Beach, Information Office. "Huntington Beach Library—'Simple Bold Glazed Pavilion . . .'" *California Librarian* (January 1975): 46–49.

City of Sydney. "How the Jury Chose the Winner of Our Green Square Library and Plaza Design Competition." YouTube video, published February 25, 2013. www.youtube.com/watch?v=qVABfj2lSGY.

Cottrell, Megan. "Baltimore's Library Stays Open During Unrest." *American Libraries*, May 1, 2015. https://americanlibrariesmagazine.org/blogs/the-scoop/qa-carla-hayden-baltimore.

County of Marin. "Marin County Civic Center: Designed by Frank Lloyd Wright." MarinCounty.org, n.d. www.marincounty.org/depts/cu/history.

Cummins, Tori Masucci. "Home Grown." *Sactown Magazine* (December–January 2017). www.sactownmag.com/December-January-2017/Home-Grown.

Dalglish, Brenda. "Bio-Wall at College Library More Than 'Pretty Plants.'" *The Globe and Mail*, April 30, 2018. www.theglobeandmail.com/report-on-business/industry-news/property-report/bio-wall-at-college-library-more-than-pretty-plants/article4490142.

D'Andre, Joey. "Final Project: Davis Bilingual Magnet School Community Garden." YouTube video, published April 29, 2014. www.youtube.com/watch?v=sDSI-NMPWvw.

Dawson, Gloria. "5 Public Libraries That Have Gone to Seed (Libraries)." *Modern Farmer*, July 17, 2013. https://modernfarmer.com/2013/07/5-public-libraries-that-have-gone-to-seed-libraries.

Delgado-LaStella, Tracy, and Sandra Feinberg. "The Nature Explorium." *Networking*, July 10, 2010. www.natureexplorium.org/pdfs/671%20Networking%20July%202010%20-%20Nature%20Explorium.pdf.

Delsesto, Matthew. "Inside Rikers Island with the Jail-to-Street GreenHouse Program by the Horticultural Society of New York." *Untapped Cities*, November 20, 2013. https://untappedcities.com/2013/11/20/inside-rikers-island-jail-to-street-greenhouse-program-by-horticultural-society-new-york.

Department of Horticulture. "Display Garden." Washington State University, College of Agricultural, Human, and Natural Resource Sciences, n.d. horticulture.wsu.edu/gardens-orchards/display-garden.

Donaldson, Jesse. "The Vancouver Public Library Green Roof." *Montecristo Magazine*, August 25, 2017. http://montecristomagazine.com/community/vancouver-public-library-green-roof.

Dumbarton Oaks Archives. "The Victory Garden." Dumbarton Oaks Research Library and Collection blog, June 15, 2017. www.doaks.org/research/library-archives/dumbarton-oaks-archives/historical-records/75th-anniversary/blog/the-victory-garden.

Dusenbery, Paul B. "The STEM Education Movement in Public Libraries." InformalScience.org, October 1, 2013. www.informalscience.org/stem-education-movement-public-libraries.

Dwire, Patrick. "Felton Library Scheduled to Break Ground in Late Summer." *Press Banner*, May 9, 2018. www.goldenstatenewspapers.com/press_banner/felton-library-scheduled-to-break-ground-in-late-summer/article_de253e46-53da-11e8-884f-73489e9cd4c6.html.

Dybas, Cheryl, and Mick Kulikowski. "Shrinking Habitats Have Adverse Effects on World Ecosystems—and Ultimately People." NSF.org: Discovery, March 23, 2015. https://nsf.gov/discoveries/disc_summ.jsp?cntn_id=134468&org=NSF.

Eaton, Joe, and Ron Sullivan. "Children's Garden Takes Root at S.F. Library." *SFGate*, December 20, 2009. www.sfgate.com/homeandgarden/article/Children-s-garden-takes-root-at-S-F-library-3277831.php.

Edwards, Bonnie. "Library's Community Garden to Receive Grant." *The Goldsboro News-Argus*, February 27, 2008. www.newsargus.com/news/archives/2008/02/27/librarys_community_garden_to_receive_grant (page no longer active).

Epting, Chris. "In the Pipeline: Timeless Design Has Helped Huntington Beach Library Stand Test of Time." *Los Angeles Times*, April 15, 2015. www.latimes.com/socal/hb-independent/opinion/tn-hbi-me-0416-pipeline-20150414-story.html.

Etherington, Natasha. *Gardening for Children with Autism Spectrum Disorders and Special Education Needs: Engaging with Nature to Combat Anxiety, Promote Sensory Integration and Build Social Skills*. London: Jessica Kingsley, 2012.

Falk, John H., and Lynn D. Dierking. "The 95 Percent Solution." *American Scientist* (November–December 2010): 486–93.

Fargas Malet, M., D. McSherry, E. Larkin, and C. Robinson. "Research with Children: Methodological Issues and Innovative Techniques." *Journal of Early Childhood Research* 8, no. 2 (2010): 175–92. https://pure.qub.ac.uk/ws/files/13808523/Research_with_children_methodological_issues_and_innovative_techniques.pdf.

Feddern, Donna. "Community Garden Engages Homeless Patrons and Non-Profit Neighbors." Washington Library Association/WLA.org, n.d. https://wala.memberclicks.net/community-garden-engages-homeless-patrons-and-non-profit-neighbors.

Federal Writers Project of the Works Progress Administration. *Los Angeles in the 1930s: The WPA Guide to the City of Angels*. Berkeley: University of California Press, 2011.

Filby, Max. "UD Library to Feature Indoor 'Living Garden' Exhibit." *Dayton Daily News*, March 20, 2017. www.daytondailynews.com/news/library-feature-indoor-living-garden-exhibit/EePsOnO81OjZAHadq5WxzH.

Fine, Jud, and Harry Reese. *Spine: An Account of the Jud Fine Art Plan at the Maguire Gardens Central Library, Los Angeles*. Los Angeles: Los Angeles Library Association, 1993.

Florida, Richard. "It's Not the Food Deserts: It's the Inequality." *City Lab*, January 18, 2018. www.citylab.com/equity/2018/01/its-not-the-food-deserts-its-the-inequality/550793.

Fogleman, Lori. "Baylor Dedicates Garden of Contentment at Armstrong Browning Library." Baylor University, Media and Public Relations blog, September 17, 2012. www.baylor.edu/mediacommunications/news.php?action=story&story=122267.

Folmer, James. "Rooftop Garden Re-opens as Library Celebrates 10 Years." *Highland Community News*, May 9, 2018. www.highlandnews.net/news/rooftop-garden-re-opens-as-library-celebrates-years/article_32331f02-53dc-11e8-b32b-d3b15e741034.html.

Friends of Birmingham Botanical Gardens. "Education and Selected Programs for the Period July 1, 2014–June 30, 2015." BBGardens.org, September 16, 2015. www.bbgardens.org/documents/EducationReportFinal2015.pdf.

Friends of the Saint Paul Public Library, The. "Library Wins Environmental Initiative Award for Nature-Smart Partnership." TheFriends.org, May 30, 2016. https://thefriends.org/2016/05/30/library-wins-environmental-initiative-award-for-nature-smart-partnership.

GAEA Project. "The GAEA Project By-Laws." The University of North Carolina at Chapel Hill, n.d. https://heellife.unc.edu/organization/thegaeaproject/documents/view/472685.

Gardner, Howard. *Frames of Mind: The Theory of Multiple Intelligences*. New York: Basic Books, 2011.
Ghoting, Saroj. "The Five Practices and the Early Literacy Components Support Each Other." EarlyLit.net, n.d. http://static1.squarespace.com/static/531bd3f2e4b0a09d95833 bfc/t/568c4ba3bfe87399730708f2/1452034979939/elcomppracchart.pdf.
Gibby, David, William Scheer, Sharon Collmen, and George Pinyuh. "The Master Gardener Program: A WSU Extension Success Story; Early History From 1973." Washington State University, 2008. http://web.archive.org/web/20100531193151/http://ferry.wsu.edu/ gardening/MasterGardenerProgramHistory.pdf.
Gillespie, Marianne. "Library Group Greening Grounds." *Chillicothe Times-Bulletin*, July 20, 2011. www.chillicothetimesbulletin.com/article/20110720/NEWS/307209994.
Gillingham, Olivia, and Kayla Harris. "Mary's Gardens Movement Lives On." Marian Library blog, May 8, 2018. https://udayton.edu/blogs/imri/2018-05-08-marys-garden-movement -lives-on.php.
Glen, Charlotte D., Gary E. Moore, K. S. U. Jayaratne, and Lucy K. Bradley. "Characteristics of Extension Demonstration Gardens."*Journal of Extension* (April 2013). www.joe.org/ joe/2013april/rb8.php.
———. "Use of Demonstration Gardens in Extension: Challenges and Benefits." *Journal of Extension* (August 2014). www.joe.org/joe/2014august/a6.php.
Grant, Amy. "What Is a Reading Garden: How to Create a Reading Nook in Gardens." Gardening KnowHow.com, April 4, 2018. www.gardeningknowhow.com/special/spaces/reading -garden-design.htm.
Grant, Samantha. "'Butterflies' Sculpture Installed Outside Central Library." *5 on Your Side*, April 12, 2017. www.ksdk.com/article/news/local/butterflies-sculpture-installed-outside -central-library/430798693.
Green Chillis Garden Club. "Thus Far: or, A Chronolog of Our Garden's First Year (Oct. 2010– Oct. 2011)." *The Library Blog*, November 4, 2011. https://cpldgarden.weebly.com/ garden-blog/archives/11-2011.
Green Engineer, The. "East Boston Branch: Boston Public Library." GreenEngineer.com, 2017. www.greenengineer.com/east-boston-lib.
"Green Thumbs at Work in Northlake Public Library's Learning Garden Project." *Franklin Park Herald-Journal*, May 21, 2018. www.chicagotribune.com/suburbs/franklin-park/news/ ct-fhj-science-kits-grant-tl-0524-story.html.
Greenberg, Gerald S. "'On the Roof of the Library Nearest You': America's Open-Air Libraries, 1905–1944." In *Libraries to the People: Histories of Outreach*, edited by Robert S. Freeman and David M. Hovde, 181–191. Jefferson, NC: McFarland, 2003.
Greenroofs.com. "National Institutes of Health (NIH) Library, Building 10." Greenroofs.com, n.d. www.greenroofs.com/projects/pview.php?id=193.
Gross, Melissa, Cindy Mediavilla, and Virginia A. Walter. *Five Steps of Outcome Based Planning and Evaluation for Public Libraries*. Chicago: American Library Association, 2016.
Harvard Library. "Gutman Library Renovation Includes Green 'Living Walls.'" Harvard Library classic site, November 6, 2012. https://emeritus.library.harvard.edu/gutman-library -renovation-includes-green-%E2%80%98living-walls%E2%80%99#.
Hayward Public Library. "From Book to Action: One Library's Story." YouTube video, published July 23, 2012. www.youtube.com/watch?v=tOkDOYR5Pb4&feature=youtu.be.
Hazlett, Denice Rovira. "Lending a Green Thumb." *Library Journal* (July 2013): 28–29.
Heos, Bridget. *So You Want to Grow a Taco?* Mankato, MN: Amicus Ink, 2016.
Hiland, Susan. "Fairfield Library Dedicates New Garden, Bench." *Daily Republic*, August 19, 2018. www.dailyrepublic.com/uncategorized/fairfield-library-dedicates-new -garden-bench.

Hillview Urban Agriculture Center. "Welcome to the Seed Library." HillviewAC.org, n.d. www.hillviewuac.org/seed-library-2.

Hopkins, Carol. "Volunteers Plant Waterford Library Gardens to Stimulate the Senses." *The Oakland Press*, September 22, 2015. www.theoaklandpress.com/news/volunteers-plant-waterford-library-gardens-to-stimulate-the-senses.

Hopwood, Jennifer. "Initiating STEM Learning in Libraries." *Children and Libraries* (Summer/Fall 2012): 53–55.

Howard County Library System. "Saving the Magnificent Monarch." Ellicott City, MD: Howard County Library System, 2015. http://d3lf1kenz29v4j.cloudfront.net/wp-content/uploads/2015/09/17093653/Monarch-brochure-Sept1.pdf.

———. "Welcome to the HCLS Enchanted Garden." YouTube video, published April 1, 2014. www.youtube.com/watch?v=FAFWQH94CZY.

Ibarra, Nicholas. 2018. "New Felton Library and Discovery Park Coming Soon." *Santa Cruz Sentinel* (May 24). www.santacruzsentinel.com/social-affairs/20180524/new-felton-library-and-discovery-park-coming-soon.

IMLS (Institute of Museum and Library Services). "How Library Gardens Are Growing Communities in Georgia." IMLS.gov: Project Snapshot, January 26, 2018. www.imls.gov/news-events/project-profiles/how-library-gardens-are-growing-communities-georgia.

"In Brooklyn, a Garden for the Bookworms." *The New York Times*, June 29, 1997. www.nytimes.com/1997/06/29/realestate/in-brooklyn-a-garden-for-the-bookworms.html.

Inklebarger, Timothy. "Library to Farm to Table." *American Libraries*, November 1, 2016. https://americanlibrariesmagazine.org/2016/11/01/library-farm-to-table.

Jiler, James. *Doing Time in the Garden: Life Lessons through Prison Horticulture.* Oakland, CA: New Village Press, 2006.

Jordan, Mary Wilkins. "Public Library Gardens: Playing a Role in Ecologically Sustainable Communities." In *Public Libraries and Resilient Cities*, edited by Michael Dudley, 101–10. Chicago: American Library Association, 2013.

Kavanagh, Ariana, Adam Rose, Cassandra Browne, Patricia Ocampo, and Lori Walsh. "Gardening Made Easier: Taking Steps Towards a Universal Design." Powerpoint presentation. [Memorial University of Newfoundland, Canada], n.d. www.mun.ca/communitygarden/Universal_Design.pdf.

Keagle, Cora L. "Outdoor Libraries." *Hygeia* (June 1938): 538–40.

Kellogg, Steven. *Jack and the Beanstalk.* New York: Morrow Junior Books, 1991.

Kelly, Stephen. "The Garden of Youthful Imagination." LandscapeOnline.com, n.d. http://landscapeonline.com/research/article-a.php?number=6807.

Kittrell, Kaye. "Long Beach Public Library Learning Garden." Late Bloomer Urban Organic Garden Show. YouTube video, published January 17, 2017. www.youtube.com/watch?v=8gxS4qM04Wk.

Klipper, Barbara. *Programming for Children and Teens with Autism Spectrum Disorder.* Chicago: ALA Editions, 2014.

Koberlein, Brian. "The Librarian and the Astrophysicist." *Forbes*, July 23, 2018. www.forbes.com/sites/briankoberlein/2018/07/23/the-librarian-and-the-astrophysicist/#78042bdd7355.

Kranz, Tammy. "Growing a Garden and a Community." *The Westminster Window*, May 21, 2013. http://westminsterwindow.com/stories/growing-a-garden-and-a-community,109960.

Kuzyk, Raya. "Learning Gardens: New York's GreenBranches Program Links the Library to the Street." *Library Journal* (October 2007): 40–43.

Landgraf, Greg. "Not Your Garden-Variety Library." *American Libraries*, January 5, 2015. https://americanlibrariesmagazine.org/2015/01/05/not-your-garden-variety-library.

Lane, Dexter. "Anythink Libraries: Experiential Learning Indoors and Out." NatureExplore.org, August 20, 2015. https://natureexplore.org/anythink-libraries-experiential-learning-indoors-and-out.

Langellotto, Gail Ann, David Moen, Terry Straub, and Sheri Dorn. "The First Nationally Unifying Mission Statement and Program Standards for Extension Master Gardener Programs at Land-Grant Universities." *Journal of Extension* 53, no. 1 (2015). www.joe.org/joe/2015February/iw1.php.

Lankes, R. David. "Expect More: Why Libraries Cannot Become STEM Educators." R. David Lankes website, August 21, 2015. https://davidlankes.org/expect-more-why-libraries-cannot-become-stem-educators.

Lasnier, Guy. "Puma Tracking Reveals Impact of Habitat Fragmentation." University of California, April 18, 2013. www.universityofcalifornia.edu/news/puma-tracking-reveals-impact-habitat-fragmentation.

LaTrace, A. J. "16 of Chicago's Greatest Secret Gardens and Park Spaces." CurbedChicago.com, August 17, 2015. https://chicago.curbed.com/maps/chicago-secret-gardens-map.

Laylin, Tafline. "The Semiahmoo Library's Larger Than Life Living Wall Features Over 10,000 Plants." Inhabitat.com, August 30, 2011. https://inhabitat.com/the-semiahmoo-librarys-larger-than-life-living-wall-features-over-10000-plants.

Le, Sarah Roullard. "A Neutra Gem in Huntington Beach—Central Library." BetterLivingSoCal.com, 2018. http://betterlivingsocal.com/a-neutra-gem-in-huntington-beach-central-library.

Lehmkuhl, John. "Wildlife Habitat Fragmentation." *Western Forester* (November/December 2005): 8–9. www.fs.fed.us/pnw/pubs/journals/pnw_2005_lehmkuhl001.pdf.

Lehn, Carla Campbell. "Finding and Keeping Good Volunteers: From Recruitment to Sustainability." In *Library Volunteers Welcome! Strategies for Attracting, Retaining and Making the Most of Willing Helpers*, edited by Carol Smallwood and Laura Sanborn, 33–41. Jefferson, NC: McFarland, 2016.

Leibel, Dan. "DDC Cuts Ribbon in New Garden at Park Slope Library." NYC Department of Design and Construction, May 8, 2017. www1.nyc.gov/site/ddc/about/press-releases/2017/pr-050817-ribbon-cutting.page.

LibraryFarm. "LibraryFarm Rules and Responsibilities 2017." [Cicero, NY: Northern Onondaga Public Library], 2017. www.nopl.org/wp-content/uploads/2014/11/2017-Rules-and-Responsibilities.pdf.

Liebergen, Leah. "Growing a Library Edible Garden: Tales from the Brown County Library's Cellcom Children's Edible Garden." Webinar. [Green Bay, WI: Nicolet Federated Library System], n.d. www.nfls.lib.wi.us/uploads/5/5/1/3/55139073/garden_webinar_updated.pdf.

Lindsay. "Huntington Beach Central Library and Cultural Center from 'Rosewood.'" IAMNOTASTALKER.com, May 3, 2017. www.iamnotastalker.com/2017/05/03/huntington-beach-central-library-and-cultural-center-from-rosewood.

Los Angeles Public Library. "Early History, Design and Construction of the Goodhue Building." LAPL.org, n.d. www.lapl.org/branches/central-library/art-architecture/goodhue-building.

Louv, Richard. "Five Ways Libraries Can Apply the Nature Principle." *Psychology Today*, March 9, 2011a. www.psychologytoday.com/us/blog/people-in-nature/201103/five-ways-libraries-can-apply-the-nature-principle-0.

———. "Naturebraries: How Libraries Can Connect Children and Adults to Nature and Build Support for Libraries." Children & Nature Network, March 2, 2011b. www.childrenandnature.org/2011/03/02/how-libraries-can-connect-children-and-adults-to-nature.

Lummis, Charles F. *Los Angeles Public Library: Eighteenth Annual Report for the Year Ending November 30, 1906.* Los Angeles: Times-Mirror Printing and Binding House, 1907.
Lynch, Grace Hwang. "Dig It!" *School Library Journal* (August 2014): 24–27.
Macaulay, David. "Thirteen Studios: 2008 May Hill Arbuthnot Honor Lecture." *Children and Libraries* (Summer/Fall 2009): 9–15.
Madison Public Library. "Sustainability Partnerships at Madison Public Library: Central Library Goes Green." MadisonPublicLibrary.org, n.d. www.madisonpubliclibrary.org/engagement/green.
"Maguire Gardens—Los Angeles Central Library." *Landscape Voice*, December 13, 2012. http://landscapevoice.com/maguire-gardens-los-angeles-central-library.
Marin Master Gardeners. "Community Gardens." University of California, Division of Agriculture and Natural Resources, 2018. http://marinmg.ucanr.edu/Great_Gardening_Information/Marin_Community_Gardens/#.
Mark, Joshua J. "Labyrinth." In *Ancient History Encyclopedia*. Definition published April 16, 2018. www.ancient.eu/Labyrinth.
Marpillero Pollak Architects (MPA). "GreenBranches Library Learning Gardens." MPA Portfolio—Institutional, n.d. http://mparchitectsnyc.com/sites/mpa/files/GB_Greenbranches LearningGardens.pdf.
Master Gardeners of Benton and Franklin Counties. "The Place to Grow." Washington State University Extension, n.d. https://extension.wsu.edu/benton-franklin/mastergardeners/our-programs/demogarden.
Master Gardeners of Northern Virginia (MGNV). "Glencarlyn Library Community Garden." MGNV.org, n.d. https://mgnv.org/demonstration-gardens-2/glencarlyn-library-community-garden.
McCammond-Watts, Heather. "Can You Dig It? Library Gardens Are Growing in Illinois." *ILA Reporter* XXXIII, no. 6 (December 2015). www.ila.org/publications/ila-reporter/article/18/can-you-dig-it-library-gardens-are-growing-in-illinois.
McCormack, Aoife. *Learning through Gardening Course: A Resource Pack for Adult Literacy Tutors.* Dublin, Ireland: National Adult Literacy Agency, 2014. https://nala.ie/resources/kerry-etb-learning-through-gardening-level-2.
Mediavilla, Cynthia Lou. "Carma Russell (Zimmerman) Leigh—An Historical Look at a Woman of Vision and Influence." PhD dissertation, University of California, Los Angeles, 2000.
Meinhold, Bridgette. "Mexico City Public Library Surrounded by Botanical Garden." Inhabitat.com, December 27, 2010. https://inhabitat.com/mexico-city-public-library-surrounded-by-botanical-garden.
Meyer, Leila. "STEM and the Standards: Librarians, Maker Spaces, and the NGSS." *School Library Journal* (January 2018): 34–36.
Meyers, Alex. "Westbank Community Garden." Westbank Libraries, 2017. www.westbanklibrary.com/community-garden.
Miller, Joan. "Landa Community Garden." Monte Vista Historical Association, *News Blog*, October 9, 2015. www.montevista-sa.org/news-blog/item/landa-community-garden.
Mills, Elaine. "Meet the Glencarlyn Library Community Garden Coordinators." Master Gardeners of Northern Virginia/MGNV.org, February 28, 2018. https://mgnv.org/2018/02/28/meet-the-glencarlyn-library-community-garden-coordinators.
Mills, Sarah. "Library Is No Longer Just for Readers." MySA.com, June 17, 2012. www.mysanantonio.com/news/local_news/article/Library-is-no-longer-just-for-readers-3640773.php#ixzz1yCE7bJPi.

Modin, Melanie. "The Magical, Medicinal NLM Herb Garden." *NLM in Focus*, June 1, 2017. https://infocus.nlm.nih.gov/2017/06/01/the-magical-medicinal-nlm-herb-garden.

Montgomery, Alicia, and Emily Bredberg. "How to Put the Library in STEM." Webinar, Association for Library Service to Children, April 29, 2015. www.ala.org/alsc/stem-at-your-library.

Morris, Edwin T. *The Gardens of China: History, Art, and Meanings*. New York: Charles Scribner's Sons, 1983.

Mountain Plains Library Association. "New Mexico." *MPLA Newsletter* (December 2014–January 2015): 19–20. http://mpla.us/about/announcements/newsletter-201412.pdf.

Mt. Lebanon Public Library. "Mt. Lebanon Public Library 2012 Annual Report." MtLebanonLibrary.org, 2012. http://mtlebanonlibrary.org/ArchiveCenter/ViewFile/Item/48.

National Geographic Society. "Xeriscaping." Encyclopedic entry, NationalGeographic.org, n.d. www.nationalgeographic.org/encyclopedia/xeriscaping.

National Library Board (NLB), Singapore. "National Library Building." NLB.gov.sg, March 21, 2018. www.nlb.gov.sg/VisitUs/NationalLibraryBuilding.aspx.

Nature Explorium. *Growing Nature Literacy in Libraries Resource Book*. Centereach, NY: Middle Country Public Library, n.d. www.natureexplorium.org/pdfs/Growing%20Nature%20Literacy%20in%20Libraries%20Resource%20Book.pdf.

Neary, Lynn. "Talk, Sing, Read, Write, Play: How Libraries Reach Kids Before They Can Read." NPR.org, December 30, 2014. www.npr.org/2014/12/30/373783189/talk-sing-read-write-play-how-libraries-reach-kids-before-they-can-read.

Neuman, Susan B., Naomi Moland, and Donna Celano. *Bringing Literacy Home: An Evaluation of the Every Child Ready to Read Program*. Chicago: American Library Association, 2017. http://everychildreadytoread.org/wp-content/uploads/2017/11/2017-ECRR-Report-Final.pdf.

Neutra, Dion. "The Neutra Genius: Innovations and Vision." *Modernism* 1, no. 3 (1998). http://neutra.org/the-neutra-genius-innovations-vision.

NOAA (National Oceanic and Atmospheric Administration) Fisheries. "Habitat Conservation: Reopening Rivers for Migratory Fish." NOAA.gov, accessed June 7, 2018. www.fisheries.noaa.gov/national/habitat-conservation/reopening-rivers-migratory-fish.

Oakland Public Library. "Tool List & Lending Guidelines." OaklandLibrary.org, n.d. www.oaklandlibrary.org/locations/tool-lending-library/tool-list-lending-guidelines.

"Of Library Activities in Kansas." *Kansas Library Bulletin* 16 (June–September 1947): 16.

Office of Sustainability, City of Austin, Texas. "Talk Green to Me: The Central Library." Facebook video, published July 23, 2018. www.facebook.com/austinsustainability/videos/1476436975790230.

Orlean, Susan. *The Library Book*. New York: Simon & Schuster, 2018.

Otto, Marjorie. "Sun Ray Connects Youth to Reading and Nature." *LillieNews*, June 26, 2016. www.bulletin-news.com/articles/2016/06/26/sun-ray-library-connects-youth-reading-and-nature.

Page, Lane. "Miller Libraries Enchanted Garden." *Howard County Times*, April 29, 2014. www.baltimoresun.com/news/maryland/howard/howard-magazine/bs-exho-miller-libraries-enchanted-garden-20140429-story.html.

"Park Sitters Shun Open-Air Library." *New York Times*, August 18, 1935.

Parr, Rebecca. "Oakland's Community Toolbox." *East Bay Times*, January 25, 2017. www.eastbaytimes.com/2017/01.20/oaklands-community-toolbox.

Pascoe, Joanne, and Claire Wyatt-Smith "Curriculum Literacies and the School Garden." *Literacy Learning: The Middle Years* 21, no. 1 (2013): 34–47. https://research-repository.griffith.edu.au/bitstream/handle/10072/56446/90156_1.pdf?sequence=1&isAllowed=y.

Penick, Pam. "New Central Library—'Austin's Front Porch'—Boasts Rooftop Garden and More." *Digging* (blog), December 15, 2017. www.penick.net/digging/?p=45983.

Pfahl, Carla, and Beth Staats. "Metropolitan State University's Labyrinth Garden." *Minitex News*, April 30, 2014. https://news.minitex.umn.edu/news/reference-outreach-instruction/metropolitan-state-university-library%E2%80%99s-labyrinth-garden.

Pierce, Jennifer Burek. "Grassroots Report: One of the 'World's Most Beautiful Libraries.'" *American Libraries* (May 2004): 55.

Placitas Community Library. "Placitas Library Gardens." PlacitasLibrary.com, n.d. http://placitaslibrary.com/library-activities/placitas-library-gardens.

Powe, André R. "Empowered and Empowering: Library Outreach with Older Volunteers." In *Library Volunteers Welcome! Strategies for Attracting, Retaining and Making the Most of Willing Helpers*, edited by Carol Smallwood and Laura Sanborn, 145–51. Jefferson, NC: McFarland, 2016.

Power, Effie L. *Work with Children in Public Libraries*. Chicago: American Library Association, 1943.

Pranis, Eve. "Linking Literacy and Garden Creatures." The National Gardening Association Learning Library, n.d. https://garden.org/learn/articles/view/1731 (URL no longer active).

Project Outcome. "Project Outcome: Follow-Up Survey Protocol." Public Library Association, 2017. www.projectoutcome.org/surveys-resources/follow-up-survey-protocol.

"Pupils Shun Movies and Gum to Build Fitchburg Library." *Christian Science Monitor*, July 9, 1947.

"Report of the Director, 1906." *Bulletin of the New York Public Library* 10 (October 1906).

Richmond Grows. "Richmond Grows Seed Lending Library." RichmondGrowsSeeds.org, n.d. www.richmondgrowsseeds.org/create-a-library.html.

Riley, Seth P. D., Laurel E. K. Serieys, John P. Pollinger, Jeffrey A Sikich, Lisa Dalbeck, Robert K. Wayne, and Holly B. Ernest. "Individual Behaviors Dominate the Dynamics of an Urban Mountain Lion Population Isolated by Roads." *Current Biology*, August 14, 2014. www.cell.com/current-biology/fulltext/S0960-9822(14)00855-0.

Robison, Mark. "Downtown Reno Library Named 'Coolest Internal Space.'" *Reno Gazette Journal*, April 14, 2014. www.rgj.com/story/money/reno-rebirth/2014/04/14/downtown-reno-library-named-coolest-internal-space/7712147.

Rodgers, Emily Puckett. "Great Outdoor Spaces." *Library Journal* (September 2017): 26–30. www.libraryjournal.com/?detailStory=great-outdoor-spaces-library-design.

Rosemary Garfoot Public Library (RGPL). "A Self-Guided Tour of LEED Features." RGPL.org, August 2007. www.rgpl.org/self-guided-leed-tour-pdf.

Rosenwald, Michael S. "Can Gardening Transform Convicted Killers and Carjackers? Prison Officials Get Behind the Bloom." *The Washington Post*, June 7, 2015. www.washingtonpost.com/local/can-gardening-transform-convicted-killers-and-carjackers-prison-officials-get-behind-the-bloom/2015/06/07/bf5c4cf0-0afb-11e5-a7ad-b430fc1d3f5c_story.html?utm_term=.4e7a6e29befd.

Rybezynski, Witold. "A Brand-New Olmsted." *The Atlantic* (April 2001). www.theatlantic.com/magazine/archive/2001/04/a-brand-new-olmsted/306163.

Saiger, Yael M. "Closing a Gate, Creating a Space." *The Harvard Crimson*, May 5, 2017. www.thecrimson.com/column/sketchbook/article/2017/5/5/sketchbook-8.

"Salt Lake City Public Library." Safdie Architects, 2003. www.safdiearchitects.com/projects/salt-lake-city-public-library.

Scott, Sage. "5 Reasons You Need to Visit the Salt Lake City Public Library." *Everyday Wanderer* (blog), January 4, 2018. http://everydaywanderer.com/salt-lake-city-public-library.

Seucharan, Cherise. "Vancouver Central Library's Long-Awaited Rooftop Garden Now Open to the Public." *The Star Vancouver*, September 29, 2018. www.thestar.com/vancouver/2018/09/29/central-library-rooftop-garden-now-open-to-public.html.

"Seventy-Fourth Annual Report of the Board of Directors of the Chicago Public Library 1945." Chicago: Chicago Public Library, 1946.

Smith, George Everard Kidder. *The Architecture of the United States: The Plains States and Far West*. New York: Anchor Press, 1981.

Solomon, Joshua. "Working on a Garden? GCC Seed Library Open to Public." *Greenfield Recorder*, April 17, 2017. www.recorder.com/GCC-Seeds-9230063.

Soter, Bernadette Dominique. *The Light of Learning: An Illustrated History of the Los Angeles Public Library*. Los Angeles: Library Foundation of Los Angeles, 1993.

Spencer, Roger, and Rob Cross. "The Origins of Botanic Gardens and Their Relation to Plant Science, with Special Reference to Horticultural Botany and Cultivated Plant Taxonomy." *Muelleria* 35 (August 2017): 43–93. www.rbg.vic.gov.au/documents/MuelleriaVol_35_-_p43_Spencer_and_Cross.pdf.

Starr, Ellen. "Library Garden Provides 'Rest Stop' for Monarch Butterflies." U.S. Department of Agriculture blog, December 4, 2015. www.usda.gov/media/blog/2015/12/04/library-garden-provides-rest-stop-monarch-butterflies.

Stockteam. "Huntington Beach Central Library and Cultural Center." Stockteam.com, n.d. http://stockteam.com/hblib2.html.

Suriel, Aina. "Whitestone Library Garden Gets $25K from Malba Women." *QNS*, May 13, 2015. https://qns.com/story/2015/05/13/whitestone-library-garden-gets-25k-from-malba-women.

Thielbahr, John. "Where Nature Meets Story: Get Reading Outside." Children & Nature Network, May 22, 2011. www.childrenandnature.org/2011/05/22/where-nature-meets-story-get-reading-outside.

Thomas, Erika. "Hometown Farmer: Siouxland Community Garden." *Siouxland News*, August 25, 2011. https://siouxlandnews.com/sunrise/proud-to-be-a-hometown-farmer/hometown-farmer-siouxland-community-garden.

Thomas, Sally. *Book to Action Toolkit*. Sacramento: California State Library, 2012. https://infopeople.org/sites/default/files/webinar/2015/10-06-2015/Toolkit.pdf.

Tilburt, Jon C., and Ted J. Kaptchuk. "Herbal Medical Research and Global Health: An Ethical Analysis." *Bulletin of the World Health Organization* 86, no. 8 (2008): 577–656. www.who.int/bulletin/volumes/86/8/07-042820/en.

Traver, Dorothy. "Reminiscences about the San Bernardino County Library, 1936–1974." Unpublished pamphlet, n.d. San Bernardino County Historical Archives, San Bernardino, CA.

Urban Libraries Council. "The Green Teen Garden Project @ Cupertino Library." UrbanLibraries.org, 2015. www.urbanlibraries.org/innovations/the-green-teen-garden-project-cupertino-library.

——. "Partners for the Future: Public Libraries and Local Governments Creating Sustainable Communities." In *Public Libraries and Resilient Cities*, edited by Michael Dudley, 111–26. Chicago: American Library Association, 2013.

U.S. Fish and Wildlife Service (FWS). "Atlantic Coast Piping Plover Strategic Communications Plan: Reducing Human Disturbance, 2017–2021." FWS.gov, June 2017. www.fws.gov/northeast/pipingplover/pdf/Communications_Plan_for_Reducing_Human_Disturbance_to_Atlantic_Coast_Piping_Plovers.pdf.

U.S. Forest Service. "Gardening for Pollinators." United States Department of Agriculture, Forest Service, n.d. www.fs.fed.us/wildflowers/pollinators/gardening.shtml.

U.S. National Library of Medicine. "List of Herbs in the NLM Herb Garden." NIH.gov, 2016. www.nlm.nih.gov/about/herbgarden/list.html.

Vaccaro, Chris R. "Sachem Public Library Unveils Inside/Out Garden." *Patch*, May 15, 2010. https://patch.com/new-york/sachem/sachem-public-library-unveils-insideout-garden.

"Vancouver Public Library Rooftop Garden." In *Celsus: A Library Architecture Resource*. Wikispaces.com, 2010. https://libraryarchitecture.wikispaces.com/Vancouver%20Public%20Library%20Rooftop%20Garden (site discontinued).

Vilelle, Luke. "Uniquely Lendable Collections." *Virginia Libraries* 62, no. 1 (2017). https://ejournals.lib.vt.edu/valib/article/view/1577/2148.

"Washoe County Library Listed on National Register of Historic Places." *The Record Courier*, February 25, 2013. www.recordcourier.com/news/local/washoe-county-library-listed-on-national-register-of-historic-places/#.

Webster Library. "Living Walls: Another First at Concordia." *Webster Library Transformation* (blog), September 14, 2017. https://library.concordia.ca/webster-transformation/2017/09/14/living-walls-another-first-at-concordia.

Wellman, Ruth. "Open-Air Reading Rooms." *Library Journal* 61 (1936): 667–70.

Westbank Community Garden. "Garden Agreement." Westbank Libraries, 2018. www.westbanklibrary.com/wp-content/uploads/2018/04/Garden_Agreement-APRIL_2018.pdf.

White, D'Ann Lawrence. "New River Branch Library Turns Over New Leaf with Community Garden." *Tampa Bay Online*, April 3, 2016. www.tbo.com/pasco-county/new-river-branch-library-turns-over-new-leaf-with-community-garden-20160403 (URL no longer active).

Williams, Dilafruz R., and P. Scott Dixon. "Impact of Garden-Based Learning on Academic Outcomes in Schools." *Review of Educational Research* (June 2013): 211–35.

Wilson, Matt. "Cupertino Teens Cultivate Garden at Library, Donate Vegetables to Pantry." *The Mercury News*, August 12, 2014. www.mercurynews.com/2014/07/09/cupertino-teens-cultivate-garden-at-library-donate-vegetables-to-pantry-2.

Xeriscape Botanical Garden. *Tales from the Garden*. Glendale, AZ: Glendale Public Library, n.d. http://web.gccaz.edu/glendalelibrary/Tales%20FromBook.pdf.

INDEX

Page numbers followed by *"fig"* indicate illustrations or their captions.

A

ABC Trail, 21*fig*
accessibility, 56, 60–62
active play, 40–42
Addison Public Library (Illinois), 51, 55
adult learning, 28
Alberts, Kimberly, 43
Albright Memorial Library (Scranton, Pennsylvania), 48, 49
Albuquerque Rose Society, 15, 65
Alexander, Richard, 49
Amano, Imelda, 46
America Competes Act, 24
American Association of Nurserymen's Industrial Landscape Award, 5
American Association of Seed Control Officials, 60
American Horticultural Society, 62–63
American Women's Voluntary Services, 4
Americans with Disabilities Act (ADA), 60
Ammons-Stephens, Shorlette, 83
Andriese, Paul, 48
Anythink library system (Colorado), 35, 58–59, 73
Apopka Elementary School (Florida), 23
apothecary gardens, 8
aquaponic garden, 77*fig*, 86
architectural features, 44–45
Aristotle, 1
Arlington Heights Memorial Library (Illinois), 65, 76
Arlington Public Library (Virginia), 65
Armstrong Browning Library (ABL; Baylor University), 39–40
Association for Library Service to Children (ALSC), 21, 24
audience, 46
Austin (Texas) Public Library, 47

B

Barnett, Catherine, 26
Barney's Backyard, 15–16
Bartholomew, Elizabeth, 27
Bartram, John, 1
Baylor University, 39–40
bean propagation lesson plan, 20–21, 20*fig*
behavioral problems, 23
Berkeley County Library System (South Carolina), 70
Biblioteca Nacional (Santiago, Chile), 46
Biblioteca Vasconcelos, la (Mexico), 75
Billings, John Shaw, 2
bioclimatic landscaping, 51
Birmingham Botanical Gardens, 75*fig*, 84
Blair, Kirstie, 40
blight ordinances, 59
book collections, 65
Book-to-Action, 28
Boston Public Library, 51, 52
Botanic Garden of Padua, 8
botanical gardens, 1, 74–75
Bourguignon, Mary, 72
Boy Scouts, 78
Bredberg, Emily, 24
Brenda L. Papke Memorial Sensory Garden, 39
Brooklyn Botanic Garden (BBG), 74
Brooklyn Public Library, 37, 41–42, 41*fig*, 61, 61*fig*, 74, 78, 80, 85, 91
Brooklyn Public Library's Inclusive Services, 20
Brown County Library (Wisconsin), 73
Browning, Elizabeth Barrett, 39–40
Browning, Robert, 39–40
Bryant Park Corporation, 3
Bryce, James, 4
building codes, 59

Bunting, Eve, 14–15, 22
butterfly gardens, 13–15

C
Cahalan, Sarah, 39
California State Library, 28
Canino, Adrienne, 26
canning equipment, 64
Carpenter, Novella, 28
Carroll, Edward, 33
Cellcom Children's Edible Garden, 73
Celsus, 66
Centennial College, 64
Centennial College Library and Academic Facility (Toronto, Canada), 52
César E. Chávez branch, 31–32, 78
challenges, 65–66
Charles E. Miller Branch and Historical Center's Enchanted Garden (Maryland), 11–12, 27–28, 92
Children & Nature Network (C&NN), 25, 49, 73–74
Children's Art Network (CAN), 39
Chillicothe Public Library (Illinois), 26
Chula Vista Public Library (California), 56, 57, 70
Chura, Kate, 31
Cicero Library (New York), 26, 35
colleges, volunteers from, 78
Collins, John W., 52
Common Soil Seed Library, 37
community centers, 31–32
community engagement, 31–42
community gardens, 5, 35, 57–58, 105–110
community priorities and aspirations, 85–86
Complete Herbal, The (Culpeper), 63
Comprehensive Mirror for the Aid of Governance (Ssu-ma Kuang), 1
Concordia University, 52
contemplative gardens, 39–40
Corporation for National and Community Service (CNCS), 78
Country Doctor Museum (CDM), 8
Culpeper, Nicholas, 63
Culturally Relevant Education (CRE), 17, 19–20
Cumming Library (Virginia), 22
Cupertino Library (California), 26–27
Curran, Judy, 64

D
David Barton Community Labyrinth and Reflective Garden (Saint Paul, Minnesota), 40
Davis Bilingual Elementary School (Tucson), 72, 77*fig*, 78
demonstration gardens, 5, 7–16
Deng, Cindy, 27
Dierking, Lynn D., 24
disabilities, 23
display gardens, 7
Doktor, Alicia, 55
drainage systems, 51
drip irrigation, 64
Dudley, Thomas, 47
Dumbarton Oaks, 4
Dusenbery, P. B., 23–24

E
East Boston branch, 64
Eastern Correctional Institution (Maryland), 33
Eating Local (Fletcher), 28
Ehlert, Lois, 23
El Dorado County Library (Placerville, California), 26, 65, 70, 86, 87, 89, 92
English language learning, 28
Enoch Pratt Free Library, 31
Environmental Initiative Award, 49
equitable use, 60–61
evaluating garden programs, 83–92, 88*fig*, 115–117
Every Child Ready to Read (ECRR), 21–22, 40
experiential education, 22

F
Falk, John H., 24
Farm City (Carpenter), 28
Felton Library and Nature Discovery Park (California), 70, 76

Fine, Jud, 50
Finney County Public Library (Kansas), 73
Fletcher, Janet, 28
flexible use, 60, 61
Flower Garden (Bunting), 14–15
focus groups, 88*fig*, 90
food deserts, 33, 57, 85, 92
food gardens, 33–35
Forsyth County Public Library (Georgia), 77
François Mitterand Library (FML), 74
free-choice learning, 25
French National Museum of Natural History, 74
Friend-Begin, Shawn, 46
funding, 69–72
Future Farmers of America, 34

G

Gallegos, Christine, 35
Garcia, Valerie, 66
Garden Lounge, 44
Garden of Contentment, Baylor University, 39–40
"Garden of Solitary Pleasure," 1
gardening tools, 64–65
Gardner, Howard, 18
Gateway Greening, 14
Gay, Geneva, 19
Girl Scouts, 78
Glencarlyn Library Community Garden, 9–10, 56, 72
Goodhue, Bertram, 48
Grand Rapids Public Library (Michigan), 64
Grant, Amy, 46
grants, 70
Great Depression, 3
green buildings, 50–53
Green Project of the Year Award, 32
Green Square Library (Sydney, Australia), 44
Green Teen Garden, 26–27
Green Terrace, 32
GreenBranches, 33, 48–49, 66
Greenfield Community College Library (Massachusetts), 37–38, 76
GreenHouse, 33
Greening Cities, Growing Communities (Hou et al.), 28

GreenTeam, 33
Gross, Melissa, 85
growing conditions, 62
Growing Nature Literacy in Libraries Resource Book (Nature Explorium), 65
growing season, length of, 58
GRuB (Garden-Raised Bounty), 56
Gutman Library (Harvard), 52–53
Gwinnett County Public Library (Georgia), 28, 33–34, 34*fig*, 70, 86, 87

H

habitat fragmentation, 12
Hackeling, Ann, 27
Hall Middle School (Larkspur, California), 36, 36*fig*
Halpren, Lawrence, 50
hardiness zones, 62
Harold Washington Library (Chicago, Illinois), 37, 45
Harvard, 18, 46–47, 52–53
Hayden, Carla, 31
"heat zone" map, 62–63
heat-island effect, 51
herbal medicine, 8
"Homegrown Gwinnett," 33–34
Hopwood, Jennifer, 24
Horticultural Society of Chicago, 4
Horticultural Society of New York (HSNY), 31, 33, 48–49
Hou, Jeffrey, 28
Howard County Library (Maryland), 27
humidity, 65
Huntington Beach, California, 4, 5, 44–45, 45*fig*, 66

I

Imaginarium Garden, 48
incarcerated people, 32–33
Inclusive Services garden, 61
inputs, 84
insects, 35, 65
Inside/Out, 43–44, 72
Institute of Museum and Library Services (IMLS), 33
interior gardens, challenges of, 65–66

internal partnerships, 76
interpersonal learning, 18
interviews, 88*fig*, 89–90
intrapersonal learning, 18
Irmo Branch Library (South Carolina), 13
irrigation, 11, 64

J

J. Willard Marriott Library (Utah), 51
Jefferson County Public Library Cooperative (Alabama), 74–75
Jiler, James, 33
job descriptions, for volunteers, 78
John Bowman Bartram Special Collections Library, 1
John Ester Tigg membership library (Ester, Alaska), 37
Jordan, Mary Wilkins, 55, 69, 86, 92
Junior Gardeners Club, 35

K

Katz, Bonnie, 72
Keep Michigan Beautiful award, 48
kinesthetic learning, 18
Klebanoff, Abbe, 69
Koberlein, Brian, 31
Kuzyk, Raya, 69

L

La Crosse Public Library (Wisconsin), 37
labyrinth gardens, 39–40
Lamont Library (Harvard), 46–47
land use laws, 56, 59–60
Landa Library (San Antonio, New Mexico), 10
Landstuhl Regional Medical Center, 46
Lankes, R. David, 24
Lansdowne Public Library (Pennsylvania), 69
Laramie County Library (Wyoming), 13
Laupus Library, East Carolina University, 8
learning in library gardens, 17–28
"Learning through Gardening" curriculum, 28
LEED certification, 50–53
legal considerations, 59–60
Lehn, Carla, 79
Leigh, Carma, 4
Leslie F. Malpass Library (Illinois), 44, 65, 71*fig*, 72
letter knowledge, 22
library gardens
  brief history of, 1–6
  challenges of, 65–66
  community engagement and, 31–42
  costs of, 57–59
  demonstration gardens, 7–16
  design for, 43–53
  evaluating programs involving, 83–92
  funding for, 69–72
  learning in, 17–28
  legal considerations for, 59–60
  list of, 93–104
  partnerships for, 72–76
  planning and managing, 55–66
  questions to ask when planning, 56–57
  sharing responsibilities of, 57–59
  sustaining, 69–80
  today, 5–6
  in twentieth century, 2–5
  volunteers for, 77–80
  what to grow and how to grow it, 62–64
Library in a Garden, 74–75, 75*fig*, 84
library resources, 64–65
library roles, redefining, 48–50
Library Services and Technology Act (LSTA) grant, 11, 26, 65, 70
LibraryFarm, 26, 35, 58–59
literacy programs, 21–23
literary garden, 9–10
living walls, 52–53
logical learning, 18
Long, Hope, 75
Long Island Children's Museum, 41
Lorenzen, Michael, 44
Los Angeles Public Library (LAPL), 2–3, 48, 49–50
Louv, Richard, 25, 49
low physical effort, 60, 61–62
Lummis, Charles, 2–3
Lyceum, 1
lysimeters, 51

M

Macaulay, David, 19
Madison (Wisconsin) Public Library, 51–52
Maguire Gardens, 50
maintenance, managing, 57–59
Mandela, Nelson, 33
Mānoa Elementary School (Honolulu, Hawaii), 46
Marcia R. Garza Elementary School, 32
Marian Library (University of Dayton), 39
Marin County Civic Center (MCCC), 50–51
Marquez, Amy, 32
Martinez, Mary M., 72
Mary Baldwin University, 39
"Mary's Garden," 39
Master Gardener program, 9–10, 77
mathematical learning, 18
Maurins, Arnold, 5
McIntyre, Karen, 76
measuring results, 87–91, 88fig
Mediavilla, Cindy, 85
Medical Library Association, 32
medicinal gardens, 8–9
Metropolitan State University, 40
Michelle Obama Neighborhood Library (Long Beach, California), 43, 43fig
microclimates, 62, 63
Mid-Columbia Libraries (Washington), 10, 63, 77
Middle Country Public Library (Centereach, New York), 17, 21fig, 41, 65, 69
Mill Valley Public Library (California), 11, 64, 70
Miller, Joan, 10
Million Pollinator Garden Challenge, 12
Mission branch, San Francisco, 64
Missouri Botanical Society's Project Pollinator Initiative, 14
Mixdorf, David, 57
Monarch Waystation Trail, 12
Montabono, Michelle, 37
Montgomery, Alicia, 24
Mt. Lebanon Public Library (Pittsburgh, Pennsylvania), 13, 72, 78
Mukilteo Library (Washington), 13
Multiple Intelligences, 17–20, 18fig
Murcutt, Glenn, 44

museums, 74
musical learning, 18
"mystery shopping," 91

N

Nahman-Watson Library, Greenfield Community College, 76
Napa Valley Wine Library Association, 15
narrative skills, 21
National Adult Literacy Agency, 28
National Autonomous University of Mexico, 75
National Center for Complementary and Integrative Health, 9
National Institutes of Health (NIH), 9, 32
National Library of Medicine (NLM), 9, 39, 63
National Library (Singapore), 51
National Literacy Trust, 40
National Museum of Health and Medicine, 77
National Pollinator Garden Network, 13–14
National Resources Canada, 62
National Wildlife Federation (NWF), 13
native plants, 10–12
natural learning, 18
Nature Explore Center, 73
Nature Explorium, 17, 21fig, 22, 23, 41, 69, 71, 73
Nelson, Carol, 47
Nemitz, Susan, 70
Neutra, Dion, 5, 44–45
Neutra, Richard, 5, 44–45
New River Branch Library (Pasco County, Florida), 6, 64
New York Public Library (NYPL), 2, 3
Newburn, Rebecca, 36
Next Generation Science Standards (NGSS), 24
Northern Onondaga Public Library (Cicero, New York), 64, 105–110
Northlake Public Library (Illinois), 70
nuisance laws, 59
numbers, reporting, 84

O

Oakland Public Library, 31–32, 64–65, 78
obesity, 86
observation, 88*fig*, 91
Olmsted, Frederick Law, 48
Olympia Timberland Library (Washington), 56
Omaha Public Library, 37
organic gardening, 58
outcome-based planning, 85–86
outcomes, program, 84–85, 88*fig*
outdoor reading areas, 3
outputs, 84, 87, 88*fig*, 89

P

Pace, Charles, 33–34
Pacifica-Sanchez branch, San Mateo County, California, 66
Papke, Brenda L., 39
Park Slope Library (Brooklyn, New York), 41–42, 41*fig*, 49
parks, 76
partnerships, 72–76
Pascoe, Joanne, 23
Pauma Band of Luiseño Indians library, 76
Penick, Pam, 47
"People's Garden Initiative, The," 14
perceptible information, 60, 61
permissions, 59–60
pest management, 35, 59
phonological awareness, 21
physic gardens, 8
Pittsburgh Botanic Garden, 13
Placitas Community Library (New Mexico), 40
Plaistow Public Library (New Hampshire), 78–79
planning gardens, 55–57
Planting a Rainbow (Ehlert), 23
plants
    choosing and growing, 62–64
    hardiness zones for, 62
    list of, 63
    restrictions on, 58
playing, 22
pollinator gardens, 13–15, 49
Portland High School (Tennessee), 34–35, 86

Power, Effie L., 25
Princeton Public Library (Illinois), 14
print awareness, 22
print motivation, 21
program outcomes, 84–85
Project Outcome initiative, 89
proprioception, 38
Public Library Association (PLA), 21, 89

R

R. Howard Webster Library (Montreal, Canada), 52
rain gardens, 51
rainwater, 64
Ray, Janisse, 28
"Read and Seed," 33
reading, 22
reading gardens, 46–47
Reading Room (Bryant Park), 3
Recommended Uniform State Seed Law (RUSSL), 60
results
    measuring, 87–91
    sharing, 91–92, 115–117
retention, volunteer, 79–80
Rheinland-Pfalz Library (Germany), 46
Rhodes, Bernard I., 15
Richmond Public Library, 31–32, 36
Rikers Island Correctional Facility, 33, 74
Rivington Street Library roof garden, 2
Rochester Public Library (New York), 72
Rodgers, Emily Puckett, 31
Roesch Library (University of Dayton), 39
rooftop gardens, 2–3, 5, 32, 46, 47, 51–52, 66, 75
Rosemary Garfoot Public Library (Wisconsin), 51, 64
Rustin, Jane, 83
Ryan, Rebecca, 49
Rybezynski, Witold, 49
Ryczek, Marianne, 70

S

Sachem Public Library (New York), 43–44, 72
Sacramento Public Library, 55, 57, 70

Safdie, Moshe, 47
Saint Paul Public Library (Minnesota), 49, 73–74, 76
Salt Lake City Public Library, 46, 47, 66
Sam J. Racadio Library and Environmental Learning Center (Highland, California), 52, 66
Sam W. Hitt Medicinal Plant Gardens (Chapel Hill, North Carolina), 8, 76
San Bernardino County Library, 4
San Mateo County Libraries (California), 70
Sangaree Community Garden, 70
Santa Cruz County Library (California), 70
Scarola, Rosemarie, 71
Schmitt, Donald, 52
Schneider, Hope, 38
scholar gardens, 1
school gardens, 22–23
Schoolyard Habitat, 13
ScoutingUSA, 78
seating, 46
seed libraries and exchanges, 33–38, 60
Seed Underground, The (Ray), 28
self-directed learning, 7
Semiahmoo Public Library (Ontario, Canada), 52
sensory gardens, 38–39
shade, 46
sharing results, 91–92
simple and intuitive use, 60, 61
Singh, Sandra, 47
singing, 22
size and space for approach and use, 60, 61–62
"smart drip" system, 64
SmartGarden, 11
Smith, George E. K., 5
Solano County Library (California), 72
South Sioux City, Nebraska, library, 64
Southfield Public Library (Michigan), 48
Space Science Institute, 23
Sparks! Ignition grant, 33, 70
spatial learning, 18
spiritual gardens, 39–40
Sprout Squad, 65
Spruill, Barbara, 34
Ssu-ma Kuang, 1

St. Helena Public Library (California), 15–16
St. Louis Audubon Society, 14
St. Louis County Library (SLCL), 14
Starr, Ellen, 14
Staunton Public Library (Virginia), 39
Steiner, Rachel, 37
STEM, 22, 25–28, 65, 86
Stickney Forest View Public Library District (Illinois), 26, 65, 86
Stokes, John S., Jr., 39
Storey-Ewoldt, Ronnie, 59
StoryWalk, 22
Sun Ray Library and Conway Park demonstration project, 71, 73–74
Sunflower House (Bunting), 22
sunshine, 46
surveys, 88*fig*, 89
sustainable building, 50–52
Sycamore Library (Illinois), 79

T

talking, 22
Talking Book Center, 39
Tessman, Nancy, 47
Theophrastus, 1
Three Sisters of Haudenosaunee, 72–73
tolerance for error, 60, 61
Tong, Syrilyn, 37
Tony Hillerman Library (Albuquerque), 7, 15, 64, 65, 66
tools, 64–65
tranquility, 46
Traver, Dorothy, 4

U

Universal Design for Learning (UDL), 17, 19–20, 35
Universal Design principles, 60–62
universities, volunteers from, 78
University of Arizona, 78
University of Dayton, 39
University of North Carolina, 8, 76
University of Utah, 51
University of Western Illinois, 44, 65
Urban Libraries Council, 27

U.S. Department of Agriculture (USDA), 62
U.S. Forest Service, 14

V
Van Pelt, Ann, 63
Vancouver Public Library, 47, 66
vandalism, 66
verbal learning, 18
vertical gardens, 52–53
vestibular sense, 38
victory gardens, 3–4
Villaseñor, Peter, 31–32
vocabulary learning, 21
volunteers, 77–80, 111–113

W
Walter, Virginia A., 85
wandering paths, 40
Warner Park Nature Center, 76
Washoe County Library (Reno, Nevada), 4–5, 44, 57, 66
water management, 11, 51, 64
Waterford Township Public Library (Michigan), 72
Wayne County Public Library (North Carolina), 66, 70, 83
weeds, 58
"Well of Scribes, The," 48, 50
Wellman, Ruth, 3
West Tisbury Library (Martha's Vineyard), 13
Westbank Libraries (Texas), 58–59, 64–65
Western Illinois University, 71*fig*, 72
Westmeade Elementary School (Tennessee), 13, 76, 78
Whitestone library, 71
Wildlife Habitat (NWF certified), 13
wildlife habitats, 12–13
Willner, Judith, 44
Wilson, Meg, 87
Winter Garden (Chicago), 45
Works Progress Administration (WPA), 3, 48
World War II, 3–4
Wright, Frank Lloyd, 50–51
writing, 22
Wyatt-Smith, Claire, 23

X
Xeriscape Botanical Garden, 11, 71
xeriscaping, 11

Y
Yisrael, Chanowk, 57
Young Naturalist Program, 76

Z
Zarsky, Kathy, 47
Zion-Benton Public Library (Illinois), 56, 72
zoning, 59–60